The National Statistics Socio-economic Classification

User Manual

Office for National Statistics
2005 edition

First published 2005 by
PALGRAVE MACMILLAN
Houndmills, Basingstoke, Hampshire RG21 6XS and
175 Fifth Avenue, New York, NY 10010
Companies and representatives throughout the world.

PALGRAVE MACMILLAN is the global academic imprint of the Palgrave Macmillan division of St. Martin's Press, LLC and of Palgrave Macmillan Ltd. Macmillan® is a registered trademark in the United States, United Kingdom and other countries. Palgrave is a registered trademark in the European Union and other countries.

ISBN 1-4039-9647-4

This book is printed on paper suitable for recycling and made from fully managed and sustained forest sources.

A catalogue record for this book is available from the British Library.

10	9	8	7	6	5	4	3	2	1
14	13	12	11	10	09	08	07	06	05

Printed and bound in Great Britain by
Ashford Colour Press Ltd, Gosport.

A National Statistics publication

National Statistics are produced to high professional standards as set out in the National Statistics Code of Practice. They are produced free from political influence.

About the Office for National Statistics

The Office for National Statistics (ONS) is the government agency responsible for compiling, analysing and disseminating economic, social and demographic statistics about the United Kingdom. It also administers the statutory registration of births, marriages and deaths in England and Wales.

The Director of ONS is also the National Statistician and the Registrar General for England and Wales.

For enquiries, contact the National Statistics Customer Contact Centre.

Tel:	**0845 601 3034** (minicom: 01633 812399)
E-mail:	info@statistics.gsi.gov.uk
Fax:	01633 652747
Post:	Room 1015, Government Buildings, Cardiff Road, Newport NP10 8XG

You can also find National Statistics on the internet at
www.statistics.gov.uk

Contents

List of tables

List of figures

Page

Acknowledgements

In the development of this user manual for the National Statistics Socio-economic Classification, the Office for National Statistics acknowledges the work undertaken by Professor David Rose and David J Pevalin of the Institute for Social and Economic Research, University of Essex, on behalf of the Economic and Social Research Council.

Introduction to NS-SEC

1   History and origins

1.1   Two socio-economic classifications – or SECs – have been widely used in the UK in both official statistics and academic research: Social Class based on Occupation (SC, formerly Registrar General's Social Class) and Socio-economic Groups (SEG).

1.2   In 1994, the Office of Population Censuses and Surveys, now part of the Office for National Statistics (ONS), commissioned the Economic and Social Research Council (ESRC) to undertake a review of government social classifications.

1.3   As a result of the review, the ESRC recommended that a new SEC, the National Statistics Socio-economic Classification (NS-SEC) replace both SC and SEG. (You can find full details of the review and its conclusions in Rose and O'Reilly 1997, 1998; Rose, O'Reilly and Martin 1997; Rose and Pevalin 2005. See also Related publications.)

1.4   The final phase of the review involved rebasing NS-SEC on the new Standard Occupational Classification 2000 (SOC2000) published in June of that year (see Related publications). This led to some important changes to the interim version of NS-SEC previously published in Rose and O'Reilly 1998.

1.5   Since 2001, NS-SEC has been available for use in all official statistics and surveys.

1.6   NS-SEC was developed from a sociological classification that has been widely used in pure and applied research, known as the Goldthorpe Schema (see Goldthorpe 1980/1987, 1997; Erikson and Goldthorpe 1992).

1.7   The decision to adopt the Goldthorpe Schema as the basis for NS-SEC was made because it is accepted internationally and is conceptually clear. It has also been reasonably validated both as a measure and as a good predictor of health and educational outcomes. However, NS-SEC improves on the Goldthorpe Schema with more thorough validation.

2 Conceptual basis

2.1 NS-SEC has been constructed to measure employment relations and conditions of occupations. Conceptually, these are central to showing the structure of socio-economic positions in modern societies and helping to explain variations in social behaviour and other social phenomena.

2.2 It is important that all of us who use NS-SEC understand its conceptual basis and what it is measuring so that we can use it correctly, improve our explanation of results, and investigate whether the classification continues to be valid.

2.3 Of course, a clear conceptual basis does not remove all barriers to explaining what socio-economic differences mean – employment is not the only determinant of life chances and not everything can be explained by what a classification directly measures. However, a properly constructed and validated classification such as NS-SEC removes at least one barrier to explanation. It was not designed to offer better statistical associations than SC and SEG but to improve the possibility of explaining them. As it measures employment relations, ie aspects of work and market situations and of the labour contract, it enables us to more readily construct causal narratives that specify how NS-SEC links to a range of outcomes via a variety of intervening variables (see Rose and O'Reilly 1998:27-30; Rose and Pevalin 2000:1123–5).

2.4 NS-SEC is an occupationally based classification but has rules to provide coverage of the whole adult population. The information required to create NS-SEC is occupation coded to the unit groups (OUG) of SOC2000 and details of employment status: whether an employer, self-employed or employee; whether a supervisor; and the number of employees at a workplace. Similar information was required for SC and SEG.

2.5 The version of the classification that will be used for most analyses, the analytic version, has eight classes, shown in Table 1, the first of which can be subdivided.

2.6 NS-SEC aims to differentiate positions within labour markets and production units in terms of their typical 'employment relations'. Among employees, there are quite diverse employment relations and conditions, that is, they occupy different labour market situations and work situations.

Table 1

NS-SEC analytic classes

1	Higher managerial and professional occupations
	1.1 Large employers and higher managerial occupations
	1.2 Higher professional occupations
2	Lower managerial and professional occupations
3	Intermediate occupations
4	Small employers and own account workers
5	Lower supervisory and technical occupations
6	Semi-routine occupations
7	Routine occupations
8	Never worked and long-term unemployed

For complete coverage, the three categories: Students; Occupations not stated or inadequately described; and Not classifiable for other reasons, are added as 'Not classified'.

2.7 Labour market situation equates to source of income, economic security and prospects of economic advancement. Work situation refers primarily to location in systems of authority and control at work, although degree of autonomy at work is a secondary aspect.

2.8 NS-SEC categories distinguish different positions (not people) as defined by social relationships in the workplace, that is, by how employees are regulated by employers through employment contracts.

2.9 NS-SEC distinguishes three forms of employment regulation:

- *service relationship*: the employee renders service to the employer in return for compensation, which can be both immediate rewards (for example *salary)* and *long-term or prospective* benefits (for example *assurances of security and career* opportunities). The service relationship typifies Class 1 and is present in a weaker form in Class 2.

- *labour contract*: the employee gives discrete amounts of labour in return for a wage calculated on the amount of work done or time worked. The labour contract is typical in Class 7 and, in weaker forms, in Classes 5 and 6.

- *intermediate*: these forms of employment regulation combine aspects from both the service relationship and labour contract, and are typical in Class 3.

2.10   The classification also separately identifies categories for large employers in its operational version, and for small employers and the self-employed with no employees in both the operational and analytic versions. For more information, see Chapter 6: Category descriptions and operational issues.

3 Unit of analysis

3.1 Traditionally, the unit of analysis or class composition has been the family/household rather than the individual. The nuclear family is seen as the basic structural element because of the inter-dependence and shared conditions of family members. A family member's own position may have less relevance to their life chances than those of another family member. A practical solution to this problem has been to select one family or household member as a reference person and take that person's position to stand for the whole household.

3.2 Essentially, assigning an NS-SEC category to a household involves deciding which household member best defines that household's position. This person is called the household reference person (HRP). In the past, the HRP was defined as the Head of Household: the oldest householder, with men taking precedence over women in the case of couples or non-related joint householders. Because of the overt sexism involved in this definition, it was reviewed (Martin 1995, 1998; Martin and Barton 1996) and a change agreed.

3.3 From 2001, a new definition of the HRP has been used: the person responsible for owning or renting or who is otherwise responsible for the accommodation. In the case of joint householders, the person with the highest income takes precedence and becomes the HRP. Where incomes are equal, the oldest person is taken as the HRP. This procedure increases the likelihood both that a woman will be the HRP and that the HRP better characterises the household's social position.

4 Structure and flexibility

4.1   NS-SEC can be derived in three ways – full, reduced or simplified – depending on the level of detail of the employment status information available.

4.2   The different methods allow you to apply NS-SEC to registration and other administrative data, census and survey data, and to data of varying robustness. The reduced method was developed for sources unable to collect information on size of organisation; the simplified method provides a last resort solution. See Chapters 12 and 13 for fuller descriptions of the three methods and how to derive NS-SEC using each one.

4.3   Although occupationally based, there are procedures for classifying non-employed people to NS-SEC (see 6.3).

4.4   ONS researchers have also developed a self-coded version of NS-SEC, which is suitable for use in situations such as postal surveys where the collection and coding of detailed occupation information is not justified. See Chapter 14.

4.5   NS-SEC is nested so that the operational categories offer maximum flexibility in terms of the different collapses possible (within the underlying conceptual model of employment relations) to eight, five and three analytic classes. See Chapter 7: Classes and collapses.

Classes, categories and sub-categories

5 Analytic classes and operational categories

5.1   Table 2 presents the eight analytic classes together with the 14 functional and three residual operational categories of NS-SEC. The functional categories represent a variety of labour market positions and employment statuses. They can be collapsed into the analytic classes of NS-SEC, as shown.

5.2   L14 is an optional category while L15, L16 and L17 are the residual categories that are excluded when the classification is collapsed into classes.

5.3   The operational sub-categories are required for bridging and continuity in relation to SC and SEG, rather than being necessary in terms of the conceptual base of NS-SEC. See Chapter 6 for detailed descriptions of the categories and sub-categories, and Chapter 8 for more information about continuity with SC and SEG.

5.4   The categories describe different forms of employment relations, not skill levels, so the category names deliberately do not refer to 'skill'.

5.5   Figure 1 shows how to assign the operational categories of NS-SEC to respondents.

Table **2**

NS-SEC analytic classes, operational categories and sub-categories

Analytic classes		Operational categories and sub-categories
1.1	L1	**Employers in large organisations**
	L2	**Higher managerial occupations**
1.2	L3	**Higher professional occupations**
		L3.1 'Traditional' employees
		L3.2 'New' employees
		L3.3 'Traditional' self-employed
		L3.4 'New' self-employed
2	L4	**Lower professional and higher technical occupations**
		L4.1 'Traditional' employees
		L4.2 'New' employees
		L4.3 'Traditional' self-employed
		L4.4 'New' self-employed
	L5	**Lower managerial occupations**
	L6	**Higher supervisory occupations**
3	L7	**Intermediate occupations**
		L7.1 Intermediate clerical and administrative
		L7.2 Intermediate sales and service
		L7.3 Intermediate technical and auxiliary
		L7.4 Intermediate engineering
4	L8	**Employers in small organisations**
		L8.1 Employers in small organisations (non-professional)
		L8.2 Employers in small organisations (agriculture)
	L9	**Own account workers**
		L9.1 Own account workers (non-professional)
		L9.2 Own account workers (agriculture)
5	L10	**Lower supervisory occupations**
	L11	**Lower technical occupations**
		L11.1 Lower technical craft
		L11.2 Lower technical process operative
6	L12	**Semi-routine occupations**
		L12.1 Semi-routine sales
		L12.2 Semi-routine service
		L12.3 Semi-routine technical
		L12.4 Semi-routine operative
		L12.5 Semi-routine agricultural
		L12.6 Semi-routine clerical
		L12.7 Semi-routine childcare
7	L13	**Routine occupations**
		L13.1 Routine sales and service
		L13.2 Routine production
		L13.3 Routine technical
		L13.4 Routine operative
		L13.5 Routine agricultural
8	L14	**Never worked and long-term unemployed**
		L14.1 Never worked
		L14.2 Long-term unemployed
*	L15	**Full-time students**
*	L16	**Occupations not stated or inadequately described**
*	L17	**Not classifiable for other reasons**

* For complete coverage, categories L15, L16 and L17 are added as 'Not classified'. The composition of 'Not classified' will be dependent on the data source.

Figure 1

Assigning functional and residual categories of NS-SEC to respondents

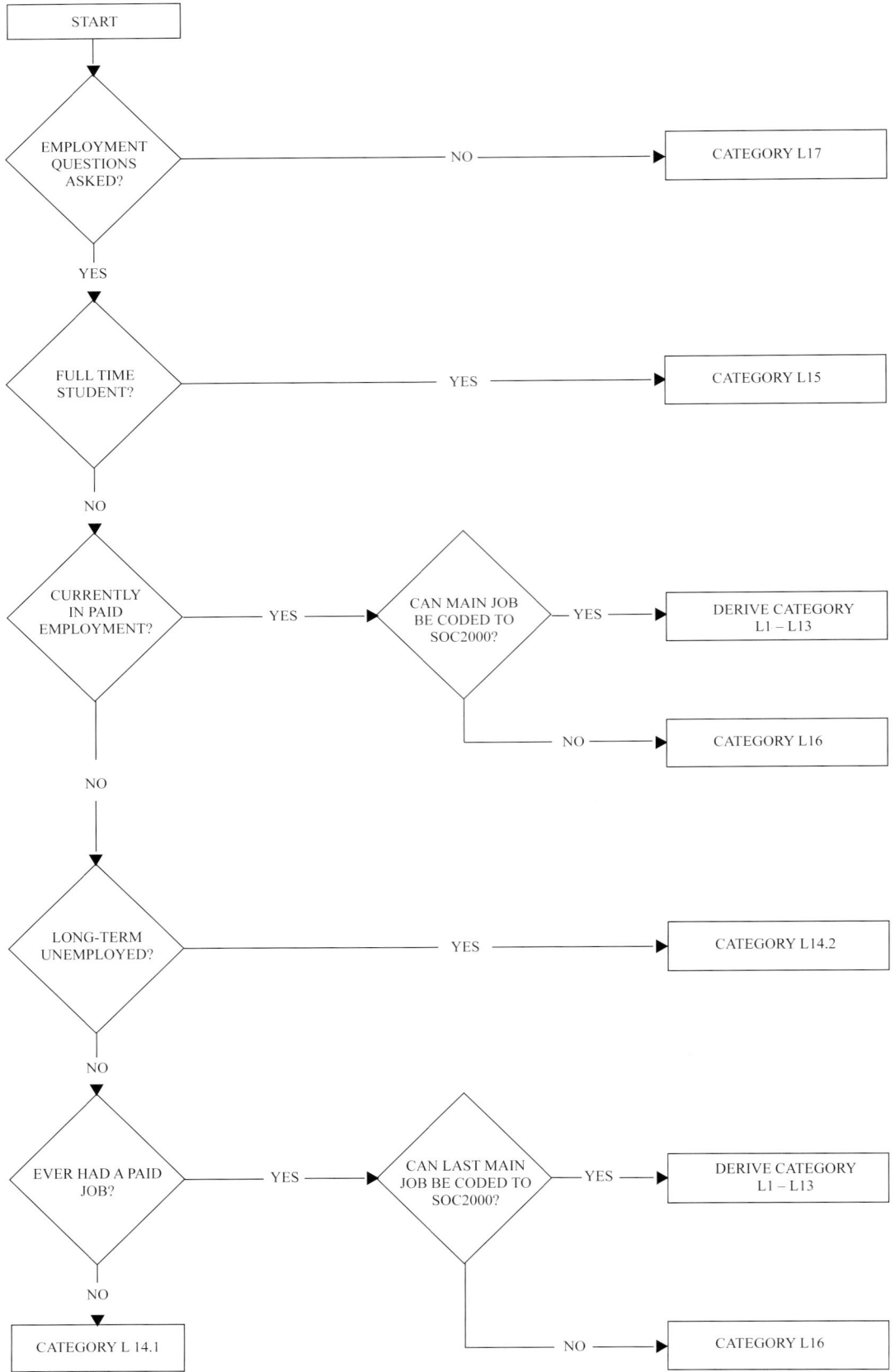

'NOTE' Long-term unemployment is usually defined as one year or over, but the period may be chosen as part of the data source definition

6 Category descriptions and operational issues

6.1   In an employment relations approach, the important distinctions are those between:

- *employers*: who buy the labour of others and assume some degree of authority and control over them

- *self-employed (or 'own account') workers*: who neither buy labour nor sell their labour to others, and

- *employees*: who sell their labour to employers

Employees are further differentiated according to the employment relations of their occupation. See 2.9 for descriptions of the main forms of employment regulation distinguished by NS-SEC.

6.2   NS-SEC has two types of operational category: functional and residual. (Residual category L14 can be considered optional.)

6.2a   Functional operational categories

L1   *Employers in large organisations*

People who employ others (and so assume some degree of control over them) in enterprises employing 25 or more people, and who delegate some part of their managerial and entrepreneurial functions to salaried staff.

Higher professionals who are also large employers are not allocated to L1 but to L3. This is because their status as professionals is more relevant in terms of employment relations than their position as an employer.

L2   *Higher managerial occupations*

Positions in which there is a service relationship with the employer, and which involve general planning and supervision of operations on behalf of the employer.

For certain managerial unit groups of SOC2000, the number of employees in an organisation can help to distinguish between higher managerial occupations in L2 and lower managerial occupations in L5. However, some managerial OUGs are wholly or primarily occupied by higher or lower managers so this does not always apply.

L3   *Higher professional occupations*

Positions, whether occupied by employers, the self-employed or employees, that cover all types of higher professional work. As with L2, employees in these groups have a service relationship with their employer.

L3.1   *'Traditional' professional employees*

L3.2   *'New' professional employees*

L3.3   *'Traditional' self-employed professionals*

L3.4   *'New' self-employed professionals*

Both here and in L4 (lower professional and higher technical occupations) 'traditional' refers to occupations regarded by SC and SEG as professional. 'New' refers to occupations not previously regarded as professional.

It is important to note that, for professionals, independent practice and salaried employment are often indistinguishable, and that true self-employment is difficult to identify.

An occupation that has been designated as professional is professional regardless of employment status. For example, a supervisor who is also a scientist is classified as a professional (in L3) and not as a supervisor (L6).

L4   *Lower professional and higher technical occupations*

Positions, whether occupied by employers, the self-employed or employees, that cover lower professional and higher technical occupations. Employees in these groups have an attenuated form of the service relationship.

L4.1   *'Traditional' lower professional and higher technical employees*

L4.2   *'New' lower professional and higher technical employees*

L4.3   *'Traditional' self-employed lower professionals and higher technical*

L4.4   *'New' self-employed lower professionals and higher technical*

Employees in category L4 share fewer of the conditions associated with the service relationship than those in L3.

The rules for allocating lower professional OUG/employment status combinations to NS-SEC are complicated. The employee relations approach holds that lower professional status takes precedence over small employer status but not over large employer status. Employers in small organisations who are in associate professional occupations are allocated to L4 rather than L8. But lower professionals who are also large employers are allocated to L1.

L5   *Lower managerial occupations*

Positions that have an attenuated form of service relationship. Employees in these groups generally plan and supervise operations on behalf of the employer under the direction of senior managers.

These occupations share fewer of the conditions associated with the service relationship than those in L2.

As discussed under L2, the size rule is sometimes used as an indicator of the conceptual distinction between higher and lower managerial occupations. However, some OUGs are regarded as inherently lower managerial and allocated to L5 regardless of organisation size.

L6   *Higher supervisory occupations*

Positions (other than managerial) that have an attenuated form of the service relationship. These positions involve formal and immediate supervision of others engaged in the intermediate occupations included in L7.

Typically, these higher supervisory positions are found in large bureaucratic organisations. Employees in these positions are supervising the work of others and so exert a degree of authority over them.

L7   *Intermediate occupations*

Positions in clerical, sales, service and intermediate technical occupations that do not involve general planning or supervisory powers. Positions in this group are intermediate in terms of employment regulation, that is, they combine elements of both the service relationship and the labour contract.

L7.1   *Intermediate clerical and administrative occupations*

L7.2   *Intermediate sales and service occupations*

L7.3   *Intermediate technical and auxiliary occupations*

L7.4   *Intermediate engineering occupations*

Although positions in L7 have some features of the service relationship, they do not usually involve any exercise of authority (other than in applying standardised rules and procedures where discretion is minimal) and are subject to quite detailed bureaucratic regulation.

L8   *Employers in small organisations*

People, other than higher or lower professionals, who employ others and so assume some degree of control over them. These employers carry out all or most of the entrepreneurial and managerial functions of the enterprise and have fewer than 25 employees.

L8.1   *Employers in small organisations (non-professional)*

L8.2   *Employers in small organisations (agriculture)*

Employers in small establishments, although they employ others, do not usually delegate most of their managerial or entrepreneurial functions to them. Small employers remain essentially in direct control of their enterprises.

The distinction between large and small employers is made by applying a size rule of 25 employees. It is likely that the majority of small employers have only one or two, or at most ten employees. Most people in this group are similar in many ways to the self-employed or own account workers in L9.

L9   *Own account workers*

Self-employed positions in which people are engaged in any (non-professional) trade, personal service, or semi-routine, routine or other occupation but have no employees other than family workers.

L9.1   *Own account workers (non-professional)*

L9.2   *Own account workers (agriculture)*

Own account workers neither sell their labour to an employer nor buy the labour of others.

L10   *Lower supervisory occupations*

Positions with a modified form of labour contract, which cover occupations included in groups L11, L12 and L13, and involve formal and immediate supervision of others engaged in such occupations.

Positions in L10 have different employment relations and conditions from those in L12 and L13 but similar conditions to those in L11. Operationally, these positions are distinguished most easily by having a job title ('foreman' or 'supervisor') from an OUG which, when combined with employee status, is allocated to L11, L12 or L13.

L11   Lower technical occupations

Positions with a modified labour contract, in which employees are engaged in lower technical and related occupations.

L11.1   *Lower technical craft occupations*

L11.2   *Lower technical process operative occupations*

Positions in this category are distinguished by having a modified labour contract. Employees are more likely than those in L12 or L13 to have some service elements in their employment relationship (for example, work autonomy). Operationally, job title does not help with the allocation of occupation to L11 as not all 'skilled' OUGs are included. Some are in L7 and others in L12 and L13.

L12   Semi-routine occupations

Positions with a slightly modified labour contract, in which employees are engaged in semi-routine occupations.

L12.1   *Semi-routine sales occupations*

L12.2   *Semi-routine service occupations*

L12.3   *Semi-routine technical occupations*

L12.4   *Semi-routine operative occupations*

L12.5   *Semi-routine agricultural occupations*

L12.6   *Semi-routine clerical occupations*

L12.7   *Semi-routine childcare occupations*

Employees in these positions are regulated by an only slightly modified labour contract typified by a short term and the direct exchange of money for effort. The category name 'semi-routine' is designed to indicate that, in employing this group, employers must slightly improve on the basic labour contract, that is, the work involved requires at least some element of employee discretion.

L13   Routine occupations

Positions with a basic labour contract, in which employees are engaged in routine occupations.

L13.1   *Routine sales and service occupations*

L13.2   *Routine production occupations*

L13.3   *Routine technical occupations*

L13.4   *Routine operative occupations*

L13.5   *Routine agricultural occupations*

These positions have the least need for employee discretion and employees are regulated by a basic labour contract.

6.2b   Residual operational categories

L14   Never worked and long-term unemployed

Positions that involve involuntary exclusion from the labour market, specifically (a) those who have never been in paid employment but would wish to be, and (b) those who have been unemployed for an extended period while still seeking or wanting work.

L14.1   *Never worked*

L14.2   *Long-term unemployed*

Both the long-term unemployed and those who have never been in paid employment (although available for work) could be treated in employment relations terms as a separate category of those who are excluded from employment relations of any kind. Operationally, however, both these groups (the long-term unemployed and those who have never worked, although available for work) are difficult to define. The problems here cannot be separated from the more general ones concerning the non-employed population.

Those who have never worked but are seeking or would like paid work are allocated to operational category L14.1. There is an argument that the long-term unemployed should not be classified according to their last job but should be assigned to category L14.2 on the grounds that they are excluded from employment relations. Therefore, when NS-SEC is collapsed to an analytic variable, you should include the long-term unemployed with those who have never worked.

It is not possible to define the long-term unemployed in any hard and fast way. You will have to make your own decisions, depending on the purpose of your research. You may not want to implement L14 at all so that you exclude the 'never worked' from the analytic versions and classify all unemployed people according to their last main jobs. Alternatively, you may want to implement the class and use a six-month unemployment rule, relating to the maximum length of time for which Jobseekers' Allowance is paid. Or you might prefer to use a one- or even two-year unemployment rule. See Chapter 10: The questions to ask.

L15   Full-time students

People over 16 who are engaged in full-time courses of study in secondary, tertiary or higher education institutions.

Full-time students are recognised as a category in the full classification for reasons of completeness. Since many students will have had or still have paid occupations, you could classify them by current or last main job, although we would not usually expect them to be classified in this way. Conventionally, where full-time students are included in analyses (for example, in research on education), they are normally allocated a position through their family household. See Chapter 10: The questions to ask.

L16   *Occupations not stated or inadequately described*

This category is for cases where the occupational data requested in surveys and censuses are not given or are inadequate for classification purposes.

L17   *Not classifiable for other reasons*

No matter what rules are devised, there will be some adults who cannot be allocated to an NS-SEC category. For example, the research may have been designed to exclude older people from employment questions. For completeness, you should include in L17 any people who cannot be allocated to another category.

6.3   The non-employed

This term includes unemployed people (except the long-term unemployed and those who have never worked); retired people; those looking after a home; those on government employment or training schemes; and people who are sick or disabled. In order to improve population coverage, in most cases, the normal procedure is to classify these people according to their last main job. The chief exceptions to this rule are full-time students, the long-term unemployed and people who have never worked (see L14 and L15).

6.4   The armed forces

Armed forces personnel are allocated to operational categories L2 Higher managerial occupations for SOC2000 OUG 1171 (officers); L6 Higher supervisory occupations for supervisors in OUG 3311 (NCOs and other ranks), and L7.3 Intermediate technical and auxiliary occupations for employees in OUG 3311.

Depending on the focus of your research and any comparability issues with the previous SECs, you can choose to exclude armed forces personnel from your analyses. If you do decide to exclude them, we recommend that you perform selection commands at the OUG level rather than on NS-SEC categories as other occupations are included in those operational categories.

7 Classes and collapses

7.1 The number of classes you use will depend on both your analytic purposes and the quality of available data. Within the conceptual model, it is possible to have eight-, five- and three-class versions of NS-SEC. Table 3 shows the nested relationship between the different versions.

7.2 The three-class version may be assumed to involve a form of hierarchy but none of the other versions can be regarded as ordinal scales. In particular, it is not appropriate to create an ordinal scale by combining the self-employed in Class 4 with the intermediate Class 3 because the self-employed are distinctive in their life chances and behaviour. We strongly recommend that you accept the theoretical and measurement principles of NS-SEC, take advantage of the conceptual base of the model for developing hypotheses linking it to outcomes of interest, and use appropriate analytic techniques for nominal data.

7.3 You should also consider carefully whether to allocate those who have never worked and the long-term unemployed to semi-routine/routine and manual occupations respectively or keep them separate. For example, if you are doing health analyses, you would need to be very careful about how you define the long-term unemployed and those who have never worked, as including the permanently sick would clearly not be sensible. They should be classified on the basis of last main job and the long-term unemployed should include only those who are seeking or available for work. Of course, this may still leave some people who are permanently sick or disabled in the 'never worked' category, hence this warning.

7.4 Although the name of the third class in the three-class version of NS-SEC is 'routine and manual occupations', NS-SEC does not perpetuate the manual/non-manual divide. Changes in the nature and structure of both industry and occupations have rendered this distinction outmoded and misleading.

Table 3

Eight-, five- and three-class versions

eight classes		five classes		three classes*	
1	Higher managerial and professional occupations	1	Managerial and professional occupations	1	Managerial and professional occupations
	1.1 Large employers and higher managerial occupations				
	1.2 Higher professional occupations				
2	Lower managerial and professional occupations				
3	Intermediate occupations	2	Intermediate occupations	2	Intermediate occupations
4	Small employers and own account workers	3	Small employers and own account workers		
5	Lower supervisory and technical occupations	4	Lower supervisory and technical occupations	3	Routine and manual occupations
6	Semi-routine occupations	5	Semi-routine and routine occupations		
7	Routine occupations	† _ _ _ _ _ _ _ _ _ _ _ _ _ _ _ _ _ _ _	† _ _ _ _ _ _ _ _ _ _ _ _ _ _ _ _ _ _ _
8	Never worked and long-term unemployed		Never worked and long-term unemployed		Never worked and long-term unemployed

* Three classes names revised 05.10.01.

† Presentation of 'Never worked and long-term unemployed' altered on Table 3 in the five- and three-class versions. This corresponds more closely to the cautionary notes in 7.2. Revised 14.01.04.

8 Continuity with Social Class and Socio-economic Group

8.1   The operational categories of NS-SEC can be aggregated to produce approximated Social Class based on Occupation and approximated Socio-economic Group (see Tables 4, 5 and 6). These approximations achieve a continuity level of 87 per cent for both SC and SEG.

8.2   In the course of rebasing NS-SEC on SOC2000, the developers produced a derivation of SC and SEG by making certain assumptions on changes over time and assessments of the relationship between SOC90 and SOC2000 unit groups. You can find this derivation on the website of the Institute for Social and Economic Research at the University of Essex (www.iser.essex.ac.uk).

8.3   NS-SEC based on SOC90 has also been developed: see Chapter 17.

Table 4

NS-SEC operational categories linked to Social Class

Social Class		NS-SEC operational categories
I	Professional, etc, occupations	3.1, 3.3
II	Managerial and technical occupations	1, 2, 3.2, 3.4, 4.1, 4.3, 5, 7.3, 8.1, 8.2, 9.2
IIIN	Skilled occupations – non-manual	4.2, 4.4, 6, 7.1, 7.2, 12.1, 12.6
IIIM	Skilled occupations – manual	7.4, 9.1, 10, 11.1, 12.3, 13.3
IV	Partly skilled occupations	11.2, 12.2, 12.4, 12.5, 12.7, 13.1, 13.2, 13.5
V	Unskilled occupations	13.4

Table 5

NS-SEC operational categories linked to Socio-economic Groups

Socio-economic Group		NS-SEC operational categories
1	Employers and managers in central and local government, industry, commerce, etc – large establishments	
	1.1 Employers in industry, commerce, etc – large establishments	1
	1.2 Managers in central and local government, industry, commerce, etc – large establishments	2
2	Employers and managers in industry, commerce, etc – small establishments	
	2.1 Employers in industry, commerce, etc – small establishments	8.1
	2.2 Managers in industry, commerce, etc – small establishments	5
3	Professional workers – self-employed	3.3
4	Professional workers – employees	3.1
5	Intermediate non-manual workers	
	5.1 Ancillary workers and artists	3.2, 3.4, 4.1, 4.3, 7.3
	5.2 Foremen and supervisors non-manual	6
6	Junior non-manual workers	4.2, 7.1, 7.2, 12.1, 12.6
7	Personal service workers	12.7, 13.1
8	Foremen and supervisors – manual	10
9	Skilled manual workers	7.4, 11.1, 12.3, 13.3
10	Semi-skilled manual workers	11.2, 12.2, 12.4, 13.2
11	Unskilled manual workers	13.4
12	Own account workers (other than professional)	4.4, 9.1
13	Farmers – employers and managers	8.2
14	Farmers – own account	9.2
15	Agricultural workers	12.5, 13.5
16	Members of armed forces	-
17	Inadequately described and not stated occupations	16

Table **6**

Social Class and Socio-economic Group linked to NS-SEC operational categories

NS-SEC operational categories		Approx Social Class	Approx SEG
L1	Employers in large organisations	II	1.1
L2	Higher managerial	II	1.2
L3.1	Higher professionals (traditional) – employees	I	4
L3.2	Higher professionals (new) – employees	II	5.1
L3.3	Higher professionals (traditional) – self-employed	I	3
L3.4	Higher professionals (new) – self-employed	II	5.1
L4.1	Lower professionals and higher technical (traditional) – employees	II	5.1
L4.2	Lower professionals and higher technical (new) – employees	IIIN	6
L4.3	Lower professionals and higher technical (traditional) – self-employed	II	5.1
L4.4	Lower professionals and higher technical (new) – self-employed	IIIN	12
L5	Lower managerial	II	2.2
L6	Higher supervisory	IIIN	5.2
L7.1	Intermediate clerical and administrative	IIIN	6
L7.2	Intermediate sales and service	IIIN	6
L7.3	Intermediate technical and auxiliary	II	5.1
L7.4	Intermediate engineering	IIIM	9
L8.1	Employers in small organisations (non-professional)	II	2.1
L8.2	Employers in small organisations (agriculture)	II	13
L9.1	Own account workers (non-professional)	IIIM	12
L9.2	Own account workers (agriculture)	II	14
L10	Lower supervisory	IIIM	8
L11.1	Lower technical craft	IIIM	9
L11.2	Lower technical process operative	IV	10
L12.1	Semi-routine sales	IIIN	6
L12.2	Semi-routine service	IV	10
L12.3	Semi-routine technical	IIIM	9
L12.4	Semi-routine operative	IV	10
L12.5	Semi-routine agriculture	IV	15
L12.6	Semi-routine clerical	IIIN	6
L12.7	Semi-routine childcare	IV	7
L13.1	Routine sales and service	IV	7
L13.2	Routine production	IV	10
L13.3	Routine technical	IIIM	9
L13.4	Routine operative	V	11
L13.5	Routine agricultural	IV	15
L14.1	Never worked	-	-
L14.2	Long-term unemployed	-	-
L15	Full-time students	-	-
L16	Occupations not stated or inadequately described	-	17
L17	Not classifiable for other reasons	-	-

How to derive
NS-SEC

9 The data you need

9.1   To apply NS-SEC to the census and social surveys, you need data on occupation, employment status and size of organisation. You can allocate an NS-SEC category by using a combination of information about:

- occupation coded to occupational unit group (OUG) level of the Standard Occupational Classification 2000 (SOC2000), and

- employment status and size of organisation, in the form of an employment status variable.

9.2   The employment status variable is created by combining data on whether an individual is an employer, self-employed or an employee; size of organisation (where collected); and supervisory status.

9.2a   Employer, self-employed or employee

You must distinguish between employers (those who employ others); the self-employed (who work on their own account with no employees); and employees (who are employed by an individual or organisation).

9.2b   Size of organisation

You must distinguish between employers in large and small establishments and, for some occupations, between higher and lower managers. To do this, you need information on the number of employees in the workplace.

As described in Chapter 6, you make the distinction between large and small employers by applying a size rule cut-off of 25 employees. Individual employers in organisations with 25 or more employees are deemed to own 'large' organisations; those owning enterprises below this threshold are classified as 'small' employers.

In government social surveys, size of organisation has been related to the workplace, ie the local unit of the establishment at which the respondent works (see Government Statistical Service 1996:45). The 2001 Census used this rule. However, it is preferable that size of organisation should refer to an 'enterprise' as defined in the Inter-Departmental Business Register (Office for National Statistics 1998:3) and not to a local unit. Local unit or workplace should be used only if it is impossible or impractical to obtain information at the enterprise level.

9.2c   Supervisory status

Supervisors are employees who are not managers but who are responsible for supervising the work of other employees.

10 The questions to ask

10.1 Two series of questions are needed in order to derive NS-SEC: three on occupation and five on employment status/size of organisation. They are designed to harmonise the collection of data across interview surveys. Other harmonised questions can be used to identify students and the long-term unemployed.

10.2 The three questions needed for coding occupation and the five for deriving employment status/size of organisation are shown here with instructions for interviewers. They are also available on the National Statistics website at www.statistics.gov.uk/methods_quality/ns_sec/questions.asp

10.2a   Occupation

Questions 1 to 3 collect information for coding to SOC2000. They ask about current job for those in paid work and about last main job for those who have ever had paid work. The exceptions are full-time students and those who have been unemployed for more than a year, who you should allocate to residual categories (L14 and L15, see 6.2b).

Question 1: Industry description

'What did the firm/organisation you worked for mainly make or do (at the place where you worked)?'

(Open)

Note: Describe fully. Probe 'manufacturing' or 'processing' or 'distributing', etc and main goods produced, materials used, wholesale or retail, etc.

Question 2: Occupation title, current or last main job

'What was your (main) job?'

(Open)

Question 3: Occupation description, current or last main job

'What did you mainly do in your job?'

(Open)

Note: Check special qualifications/training needed to do the job.

10.2b   Employment status/size of organisation

Questions 4 to 8 collect information for deriving the employment status/size of organisation variable. If the respondent answers 'Employee' to question 4, you should ask questions 5 and 6. If the respondent answers 'Self-employed' to question 4, you should ask question 7. And, if the respondent answers 'With employees' to question 7, you should ask question 8.

Question 4: Employee or self-employed

'Were you working as an employee or were you self-employed?'

1.   Employee   Go to question 5

2.   Self-employed   Go to question 7

Note: The division between employees and self-employed is based on respondents' own assessment of their employment status in their main job.

Question 5: Supervisory status

'In your job, did you have any formal responsibility for supervising the work of other employees?'

1.   Yes   Go to question 6

2.   No   Go to question 6

Note: Do not include:

- supervisors of children, for example, teachers, nannies, childminders

- supervisors of animals

- people who supervise security or buildings only, for example, caretakers, security guards

Question 6: Number of employees

'How many people worked for your employer at the place where you worked? Were there...

1.   1 to 24*,

2.   25 to 499, or

3.   500 or more employees?'

Note: We are interested in the size of the 'local unit of the establishment' at which the respondent works in terms of total number of employees. The 'local unit' is considered to be the geographical location where the job is mainly carried out. Normally this will consist of a single building, part of a building, or at the largest a self-contained group of buildings.

It is the total number of employees at the respondent's workplace that we are interested in, not just the number employed within the particular section or department in which they work.

Question 7: Self-employed working on own or with employees

'Were you working on your own or did you have employees?'

1.   On own/with partner(s) but no employees

2.   With employees   Go to question 8

Question 8: Number of employees (self-employed)

'How many people did you employ at the place where you worked? Were there…

1.   1 to 24*,

2.   25 to 499, or

3.   500 or more employees?'

*   You will need to include an additional break (1 to 9, 10 to 24) if you are intending to map the SOC2000 codes to the International Standard Classification of Occupations 1988 (COM), the European variant of the International Standard Classification of Occupations 1988.

11 Understanding SOC2000

11.1 SOC2000 has a hierarchical structure with four nested tiers. It is important to understand how this structure works before deriving NS-SEC.

11.2 The four tiers of SOC2000 are represented in the way the occupational classification codes are numbered. They are:

- Major groups – top-level, broad definitions of occupation, providing the first digit of the SOC2000 code number

- Sub-major groups – second-level definition of occupation, providing first two digits

- Minor groups – third-level definition, providing the first three digits

- Unit groups – lowest, most detailed definition of occupation, providing the complete four-figure SOC2000 code

11.3 Using the example of unit group 1211 Farm managers, Figure 2 shows how the unit groups are nested within SOC2000's hierarchical structure.

11.4 SOC2000 was published in June 2000. Volume 1 includes the structure of the classification and descriptions of the unit groups. Volume 2 contains the coding index and notes on coding. (See Related publications.)

Figure **2**

Hierarchical structure of SOC2000

Major group	Sub-major group	Minor group	Unit group	Group title
1				Managers and senior officials
	12			Managers and proprietors in agriculture and services
		121		Managers in farming, horticulture, forestry and fishing
			1211	Farm managers

12 Choosing a derivation method

12.1   There are three methods to derive the functional categories L1 to L13 of NS-SEC: full, reduced and simplified. The method you choose depends on the information you gather about employment status.

Full method

Information required: SOC2000 unit group, employment status, size of organisation

The full method achieves the best quality derivation by using all three items of information, as you can see in Figure 3.

Reduced method

Information required: SOC2000 unit group, employment status

The reduced method was developed for sources unable to collect information on size of organisation.

Simplified method

Information required: SOC2000 unit group

The simplified method provides a last resort solution: if used on its own, no records should be allocated to the first category of the classification.

12.2   At the eight-class level, the reduced method correctly allocates 98 per cent of cases compared with the full method. The simplified method correctly allocates 83 per cent of cases compared with the full method.

12.3   Tables 7 and 8 show the performance of the reduced and the simplified derivation methods compared with the full method. The data are from the 2000 summer quarter of the Labour Force Survey (June–August 2000).

Figure **3**

Employment status in the full method derivation

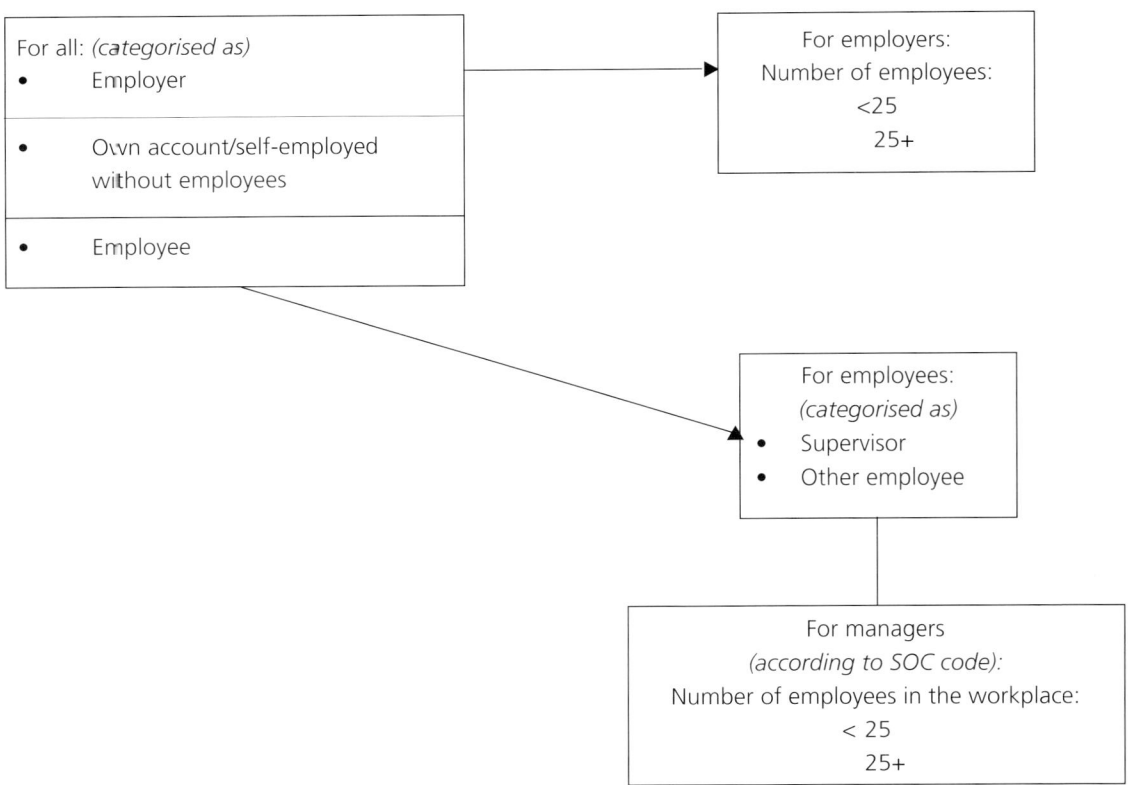

Table 7

Comparison of allocations under the reduced and the full method

NS-SEC reduced eight-class										Total	Per cent
		1.1	1.2	2	3	4	5	6	7		
NS-SEC Full											
eight-class	1.1	2877		25		84				2986	4.4
	1.2		5028							5028	7.4
	2	1164		15896						17060	25.0
	3				9227					9227	13.5
	4					6013				6013	8.8
	5						6925			6925	10.1
	6							12195		12195	17.9
	7								8804	8804	12.9
Total		4041	5028	15921	9227	6097	6925	12195	8804	68238	100
Per cent		5.9	7.4	23.3	13.5	8.9	10.1	17.9	12.9	100*	

Please note that the numbers in this table are estimates based on survey data and are thus affected by sampling and coding variance.
* Figures may not add exactly due to rounding.

Table 8

Comparison of allocations under the simplified and full method

NS-SEC simplified eight-class										Total	Per cent
		1.1	1.2	2	3	4	5	6	7		
NS-SEC Full											
eight-class	1.1	2899		51	3	22	2	3	6	2986	4.4
	1.2	17	5011							5028	7.4
	2	1164		13512	1917	467				17060	25.0
	3			18	9041	168				9227	13.5
	4	234		381	514	2934	713	427	810	6013	8.8
	5					234	3576	2164	951	6925	10.1
	6					121	44	12030		12195	17.9
	7					977	70		7757	8804	12.9
Total		4314	5011	13962	11475	4923	4405	14624	9524	68238	100
Per cent		6.3	7.3	20.5	16.8	7.2	6.5	21.4	14.0	100	

Please note that the numbers in this table are estimates based on survey data and are thus affected by sampling and coding variance.

13 Deriving NS-SEC: full, reduced and simplified methods

13.1   Many of the 26,000 job titles in the SOC2000 coding index are linked to specific industries. When deriving NS-SEC using any of the three methods, you will need information on industry from respondents in order to code occupations to the SOC2000 four-digit unit groups. See 10.2a, question 1.

13.2   To code job titles to the SOC2000 unit group 1112 Directors and chief executives of major organisations, you will need the answer to the question on size of organisation. A major organisation is taken as one employing 500 or more people.

13.2a   Using the full method

There are four steps to derive NS-SEC using the full method.

Step 1: *Code occupation to the SOC2000 four-digit unit group*

Use the answers to the questions on occupation (questions 1 to 3) to assign the four-digit unit group code of SOC2000.

If a job title can be taken as a supervisor, for the purposes of the employment status/size of organisation variable the SOC2000 code should be prefixed with an S. If question 5 has not been asked, you can use the S prefix to the occupation code in the SOC2000 coding index as an indicator of supervisor employment status.

Step 2: *Follow procedures when the answers to questions on employment status and size of organisation are missing (questions 4 to 8)*

Combine the answers to the questions 4, 5 and 6, or 4, 7 and 8 to produce the employment status/size of organisation variable. Where the questions have not been answered, take the following actions:

Question not answered	Action
4	Do not assume an answer. Go straight to step 2 of the procedure for deriving NS-SEC using the simplified method
6 or 8	Assume code 1: size 1 to 24
5	If the SOC2000 code starts with 1, no answer is required
	If the SOC2000 code does not start with 1, assume code 2: no supervisory status
7	Assume code 1: no employees

Step 3: *Derive the employment status/size of organisation variable*

The employment status/size of organisation variable has seven codes:

Employment status/size of organisation

Code	Label
1	Employers – large organisations
2	Employers – small organisations
3	Self-employed, no employees
4	Managers – large organisations
5	Managers – small organisations
6	Supervisors
7	Other employees

Use the answers or assumed answers to questions on employment status/size of organisation and the SOC2000 unit group code to derive one of the seven codes. Figure 4 illustrates the process.

Step 4: *Derive the NS-SEC category*

With both SOC unit group code and employment status/size of organisation code, use the full derivation tables to assign an operational category or an analytic class of NS-SEC.

The matrix version of the full method derivation tables (see Tables 10 and 11) contain a row for each SOC2000 unit group, a column for simplified NS-SEC and columns for the seven employment status/size of organisation codes.

Figure **4**

Deriving the employment status/size of organisation variable, full method

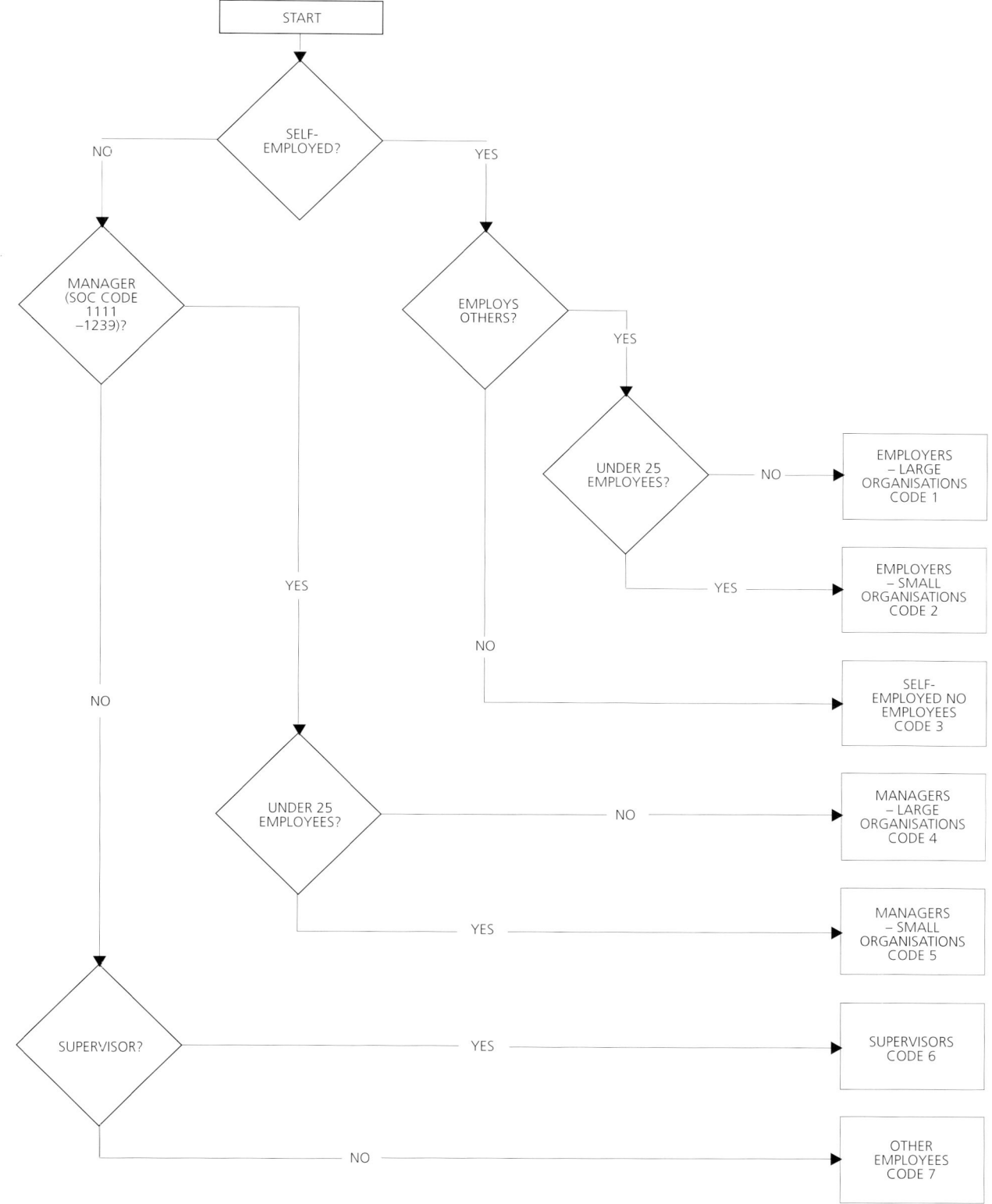

Use the SOC2000 unit group code to find the appropriate row and work across the row to reach the column for the employment status/size of organisation code. Take the NS-SEC category from the cell where the row and column intersect.

The following examples show how the NS-SEC operational category is derived using the full method:

Example 1

Question number	Question	Respondent's answers
1	Industry	Goods warehousing
2	Occupation title	Stores manager
3	Occupation description	In charge of stores
4	Employee/self-employed	1 (employee)
5	Supervisory status	[Not answered] (Not needed)
6	Number of employees	1 (1 to 24)

Resulting codes

SOC2000 unit group code	1162
Employment status/size of organisation	5
NS-SEC operational category	5

Example 2

Question number	Question	Respondent's answers
1	Industry	Stone repair service
2	Occupation title	Stone mason
3	Occupation description	Carving gargoyles
4	Employee/self-employed	2 (self-employed)
7	On own/employees	2 (with employees)
8	Number of employees	2 (25 to 499)

Resulting codes

SOC2000 unit group code	5312
Employment status/size of organisation	1
NS-SEC operational category	1

Example 3

Question number	Question	Respondent's answers
1	Industry	Dog kennels
2	Occupation title	Kennel maid
3	Occupation description	Looking after dogs
4	Employee/self-employed	[Not answered] (No assumption)

Resulting codes

SOC2000 unit group code	6139
Employment status/size of organisation	(Not derived)
NS-SEC operational category	13.5 (from simplified NS-SEC)

Example 4

Question number	Question	Respondent's answers
1	Industry	Dye works
2	Occupation title	Colour mixer
3	Occupation description	Mix colours for dyes
4	Employee/self-employed	1 (employee)
5	Supervisory status	[Not answered] (Assume 2)
6	Number of employees	2 (25 to 499)

Resulting codes

SOC2000 unit group code	8114
Employment status/size of organisation	7
NS-SEC operational category	11.2

13.2b   Using the reduced method

There are four steps to derive NS-SEC by the reduced method.

Step 1: *Code occupation to the SOC2000 four-digit unit group*

Use the answers to the questions on occupation (questions 1 to 3) to assign the four-digit unit group code of SOC2000.

If a job title can be taken as a supervisor, for the purposes of the employment status variable the SOC2000 code should be prefixed with an S. If question 5 has not been asked, you can use the S prefix to the occupation code in the SOC2000 coding index as an indicator of supervisor employment status.

Step 2: *Follow procedures when the answers to questions on employment status are missing*

Combine the answers to questions 4, 5 and 7 to produce the employment status variable. Where the questions have not been answered, take the following actions:

Question not answered	Action
4	Do not assume an answer, go straight to step 2 of the procedure for deriving NS-SEC using the simplified method
5	If the SOC2000 code starts with 1, no answer is required If the SOC2000 code does not start with 1, assume code 2: no supervisory status
7	Assume code 1: no employees

Figure **5**

Deriving the employment status variable, reduced method

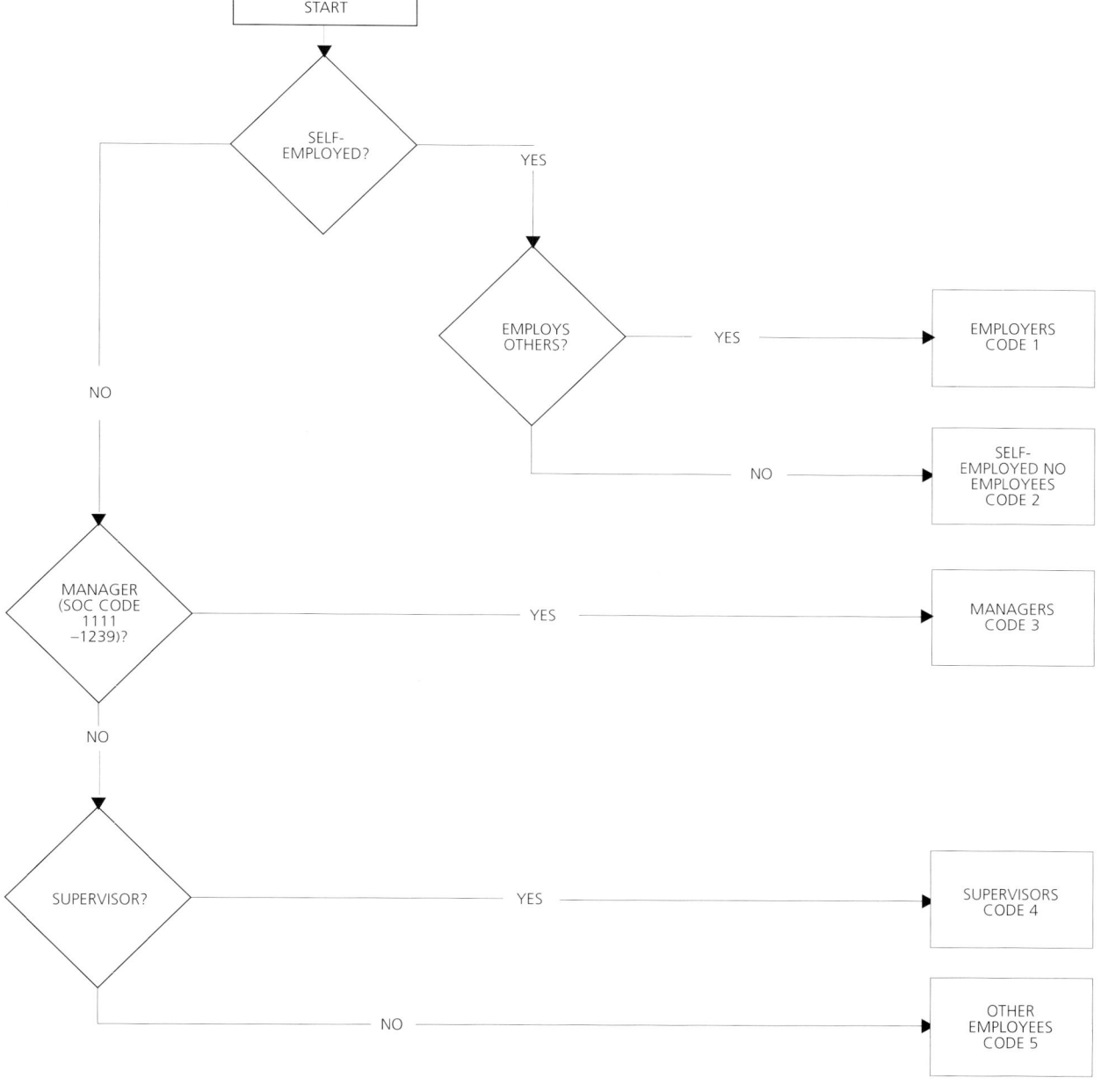

Step 3: *Derive the employment status variable*

The employment status variable has five codes:

Employment status

Code	Label
1	Employers
2	Self-employed, no employees
3	Managers
4	Supervisors
5	Other employees

Use the answers or assumed answers to questions on employment status and the SOC2000 unit group code to derive one of the five codes. Figure 5 illustrates the process.

Step 4: *Derive the NS-SEC category*

The matrix version of the reduced method NS-SEC derivation tables (see Tables 12 and 13) contains a row for each SOC2000 unit group, a column for simplified NS-SEC and columns for the five employment status codes.

Use the SOC2000 unit group code to find the appropriate row and work across the row to reach the column for the employment status code. The cell where the row and column intersect will contain a category of NS-SEC.

The following examples show how the NS-SEC operational category is derived using the reduced method:

Example 1

Question number	Question	Respondent's answers
1	Industry	Goods warehousing
2	Occupation title	Stores manager
3	Occupation description	In charge of stores
4	Employee/self-employed	1 (employee)
5	Supervisory status	[Not answered] (Not needed)

Resulting codes

SOC2000 unit group code	1162
Employment status	3
NS-SEC operational category	5

Example 2

Question number	Question	Respondent's answers
1	Industry	Stone repair service
2	Occupation title	Stone mason
3	Occupation description	Carving gargoyles
4	Employee/self-employed	2 (self-employed)
7	On own/employees	2 (with employees)

Resulting codes

SOC2000 unit group code	5312
Employment status	1
NS-SEC operational category	8.1

Example 3

Question number	Question	Respondent's answers
1	Industry	Dog kennels
2	Occupation title	Kennel maid
3	Occupation description	Looking after dogs
4	Employee/self-employed	[Not answered] (No assumption)

Resulting codes

SOC2000 unit group code	6139
Employment status	(Not derived)
NS-SEC operational category	13.5 (from simplified NS-SEC)

Example 4

Question number	Question	Respondent's answers
1	Industry	Dye works
2	Occupation title	Colour mixer
3	Occupation description	Mix colours for dyes
4	Employee/self-employed	1 (employee)
5	Supervisory status	[Not answered] (Assume 2)

Resulting codes

SOC2000 unit group code	8114
Employment status	5
NS-SEC operational category	11.2

13.2c Using the simplified method

There are two steps to derive NS-SEC by the simplified method.

Step 1: *Code occupation to the SOC2000 four-digit unit group*

Use the answers to the questions on occupation (questions 1 to 3) to assign the four-digit unit group code of SOC2000.

Step 2: *Derive the NS-SEC category*

With the SOC unit group code, use the full or reduced derivation tables for operational categories or analytic classes of NS-SEC.

In the matrix versions of both the full and reduced method derivation tables (see Tables 10 to 13) there is a column or row for simplified NS-SEC. Use the SOC2000 unit group code and the appropriate column or row for 'ssec' to find the NS-SEC category.

14 Deriving NS-SEC: self-coded method

14.1 NS-SEC is derived from occupation and employment status information, occupation being ideally coded to the most detailed level of SOC2000. As there are 353 unit groups, this can be time-consuming and costly. The five-class self-coded version is simpler and less expensive.

14.2 It is apparent that the self-coded version is not as accurate as its interviewer-coded counterpart: there is agreement in classifying only 75 per cent of cases (although some disagreement between the two classifications may arise from coder error). Nevertheless, validation exercises show that the self-coded and interviewer-coded versions display similar patterns and strengths in their relationships with other variables (for example, with smoking).

14.3 The five-class version of the self-coded NS-SEC has the following classes:

Class	Label
1	Managerial and professional occupations
2	Intermediate occupations
3	Small employers and own account workers
4	Lower supervisory and technical occupations
5	Semi-routine and routine occupations

14.4 You derive the self-coded version from a combination of information on:

- occupation (self-classified into eight categories), and

- an employment status variable that captures information on employment status and size of organisation.

14.5 The employment status variable means that you will need to know whether an individual is an employer, self-employed or an employee; the size of organisation; and the individual's supervisory status (see 9.2).

14.6 The four questions to include in self-coded questionnaires refer to the respondent's current or last main job and occupation.

14.6a Employment status/size of organisation

Ask respondents to tick one box only per question.

Question 1: Employee or self-employed

'Do (did) you work as an employee or are (were) you self-employed?'

Employee ☐

Self-employed with employees ☐

Self-employed/freelance without employees (go to question 4) ☐

Question 2: Number of employees

For employees: 'How many people work (worked) for your employer at the place where you work (worked)?'

For self-employed: 'How many people do (did) you employ?' (Go to question 4 when you have completed this question.)

1 to 24 ☐

25 or more ☐

Question 3: Supervisory status

'Do (did) you supervise any other employees?' (A supervisor or foreman is responsible for overseeing the work of other employees on a day-to-day basis.)

Yes ☐

No ☐

14.6b Occupation

Question 4: Occupation

Ask respondents to tick one box to show which best describes the sort of work they do. If they are not working now, ask them to tick a box to show what they did in their last job.

Modern professional occupations such as: teacher – nurse – physiotherapist – social worker – welfare officer – artist – musician – police officer (sergeant or above) – software designer ☐ 1

Clerical and intermediate occupations such as: secretary – personal assistant – clerical worker – office clerk – call centre agent – nursing auxiliary – nursery nurse   ☐ 2

Senior managers or administrators (usually responsible for planning, organising and co–ordinating work, and for finance) such as: finance manager – chief executive   ☐ 3

Technical and craft occupations such as: motor mechanic – fitter – inspector – plumber – printer – tool maker – electrician – gardener – train driver   ☐ 4

Semi–routine manual and service occupations such as: postal worker – machine operative – security guard – caretaker – farm worker – catering assistant – receptionist – sales assistant   ☐ 5

Routine manual and service occupations such as: HGV driver – van driver – cleaner – porter – packer – sewing machinist – messenger – labourer – waiter/waitress – bar staff   ☐ 6

Middle or junior managers such as: office manager – retail manager – bank manager – restaurant manager – warehouse manager – publican   ☐ 7

Traditional professional occupations such as: accountant – solicitor – medical practitioner – scientist – civil/mechanical engineer   ☐ 8

14.7   There are three steps to derive the five-class self-coded NS-SEC from the answers to questions 1 to 4:

Step 1: *Create the employment status variable*

The employment status variable has seven codes.

Employment status/size of organisation

Code	Label
1	Employers – large organisations
2	Employers – small organisations
3	Self-employed, no employees
4	Managers – large organisations
5	Managers – small organisations
6	Supervisors
7	Other employees

Figure 6 illustrates the procedure to follow to derive an employment status variable from the answers to questions 1 to 3.

Step 2: *Create the self-coded occupation variable*

On the basis of respondents' tick-box responses to question 4, create a variable with the following occupational codes:

Code	Label
1	Modern professional occupations
2	Clerical and intermediate occupations
3	Senior managers or administrators
4	Technical and craft occupations
5	Semi-routine manual and service occupations
6	Routine manual and service occupations
7	Middle or junior managers
8	Traditional professional occupations

Step 3: *Derive NS-SEC*

Once you have derived the employment status and occupational variables, combine them and assign one of the five NS-SEC class codes to each combination of the two variables using the matrix table (see Table 9).

If there is information missing on employment status or occupation, you can either impute missing values or treat these cases as missing data.

Figure **6**

Deriving the employment status/size of organisation variable, self-coded method

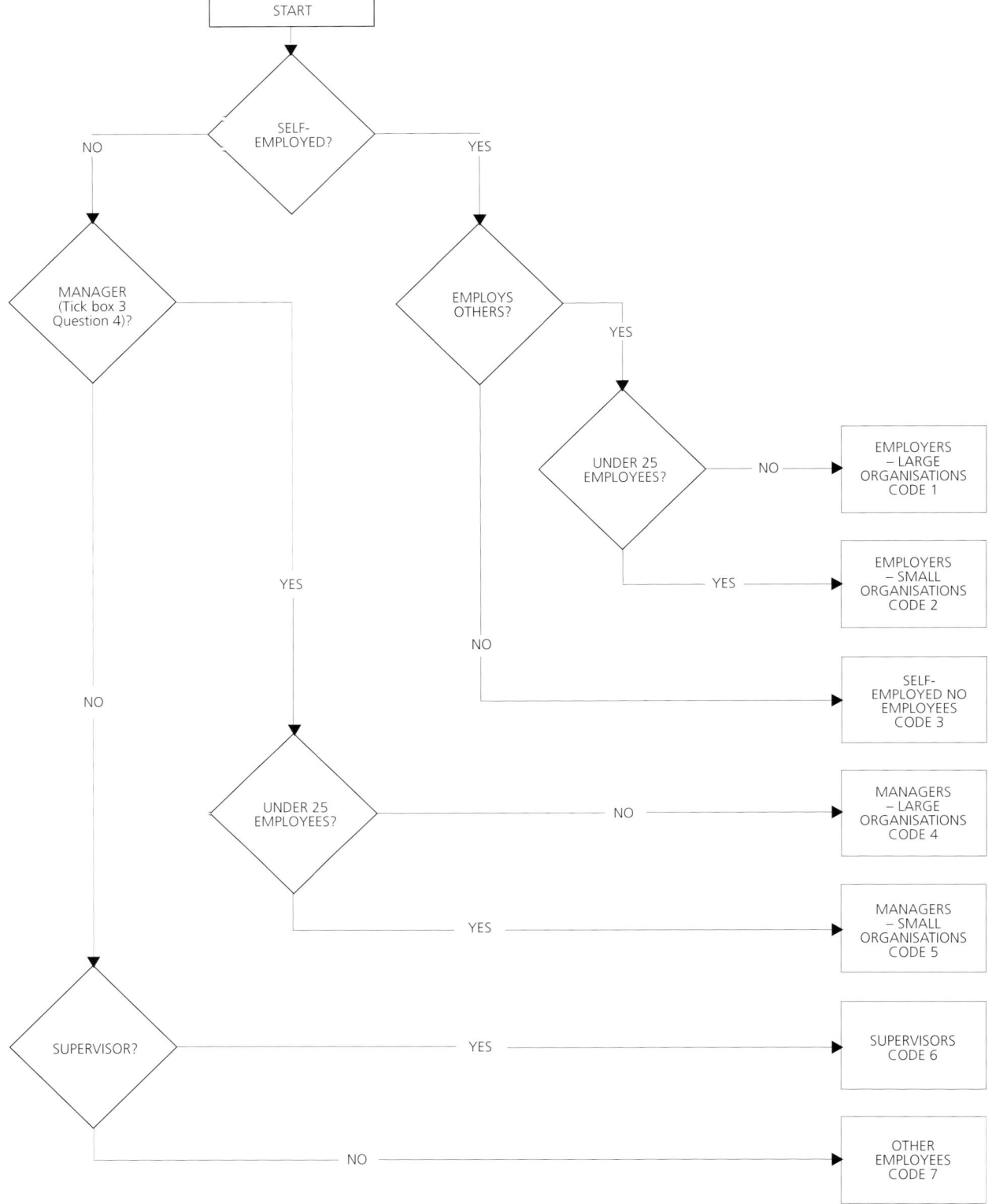

Table 9

NS-SEC self-coded derivation table: five classes

Self-coded occupation	Employment status/size of organisation						
	1 Employers – large organisations	2 Employers – small organisations	3 Self-employed – no employees	4 Managers – large organisations	5 Managers – small organisations	6 Supervisors	7 Other employees
1 Modern professional occupations	1	1	1	1	1	1	1
2 Clerical and intermediate occupations	1	3	3	1	1	1	2
3 Senior managers or administrators	1	3	3	1	1	1	1
4 Technical and craft occupations	1	3	3	1	1	4	4
5 Semi-routine manual and service occupations	1	3	3	1	1	4	5
6 Routine manual and service occupations	1	3	3	1	1	4	5
7 Middle or junior managers	1	3	3	1	1	1	1
8 Traditional professional occupations	1	1	1	1	1	1	1

The derivation tables

15 Using the derivation tables

15.1   Many users will derive NS-SEC by employing software to combine occupational unit group (OUG) and employment status. You can also use the derivation tables here. The process is similar to that used for Social Class based on Occupation (SC) and Socio-economic Group (SEG) in Volume 3 of the 1990 Standard Occupational Classification (Office of Population Censuses and Surveys 1991). which cross-classifies OUGs with employment status categories.

15.2   There are four tables for deriving NS-SEC from Standard Occupational Classification (SOC):

a) Full method – NS-SEC operational categories

b) Full method – NS-SEC analytic classes

c) Reduced method – NS-SEC operational categories

d) Reduced method – NS-SEC analytic classes

For the simplified method, use either the full or reduced method tables and look in the column or row for 'ssec'.

15.3   The derivation tables are available in two formats:

- Matrix – arranges the combinations of SOC codes and employment status codes in a matrix. This is the format used for the tables in this manual.

- Vector – arranges the combinations of SOC codes and employment status codes in a vector. This format is better for use with statistical packages such as SPSS®, SAS® or STATA®. For information on the vector tables, please visit our website at www.statistics.gov.uk or get in touch with the National Statistics Customer Contact Centre on tel: 0845 601 3034; email: nfo@statistics.gov.uk

15.4   A word of warning on statistical software: the derivation tables contain values with decimal places that relate to the operational sub-categories (3.1, 3.2, etc). With most statistical software, precision problems can arise if the variables are defined as numerical values. We recommend that you define NS-SEC variables as names rather than numerical values so that they will not be picked up by software as figures to be included in calculations.

16 NS-SEC derivation tables based on SOC2000

Table **10**

NS-SEC based on SOC2000 simplified and full derivation table: operational categories

Standard Occupational Classification 2000 unit group	Simplified NS-SEC	Employment status/size of organisation						
		1 Employers - large organisations	2 Employers - small organisations	3 Self-employed, no employees	4 Managers - large organisations	5 Managers - small organisations	6 Supervisors	7 Other employees
1111 Senior officials in national government	2	2	2	2	2	2	2	2
1112 Directors and chief executives of major organisations	2	1	1	1	2	2	2	2
1113 Senior officials in local government	2	9.1	9.1	9.1	2	2	2	2
1114 Senior officials of special interest organisations	5	1	8.1	9.1	2	5	5	5
1121 Production, works and maintenance managers	2	1	8.1	9.1	2	5	5	5
1122 Managers in construction	5	1	8.1	9.1	5	5	5	5
1123 Managers in mining and energy	2	1	8.1	9.1	2	5	5	5
1131 Financial managers and chartered secretaries	2	3.3	3.3	3.3	2	2	2	2
1132 Marketing and sales managers	2	1	8.1	9.1	2	5	5	5
1133 Purchasing managers	2	1	8.1	9.1	2	5	5	5
1134 Advertising and public relations managers	2	1	8.1	9.1	2	5	5	5
1135 Personnel, training and industrial relations managers	2	1	8.1	9.1	2	5	5	5
1136 Information and communication technology managers	2	1	8.1	9.1	2	5	5	5
1137 Research and development managers	2	3.3	3.3	3.3	2	5	5	5
1141 Quality assurance managers	5	1	8.1	9.1	5	5	5	5
1142 Customer care managers	5	1	8.1	9.1	5	5	5	5
1151 Financial institution managers	5	1	8.1	9.1	5	5	5	5
1152 Office managers	5	1	8.1	9.1	5	5	5	5
1161 Transport and distribution managers	5	1	8.1	9.1	5	5	5	5
1162 Storage and warehouse managers	5	1	8.1	9.1	5	5	5	5
1163 Retail and wholesale managers	5	1	8.1	9.1	5	5	5	5
1171 Officers in armed forces	2	2	2	2	2	2	2	2
1172 Police officers (inspectors and above)	2	2	2	2	2	2	2	2
1173 Senior officers in fire, ambulance, prison and related services	2	2	2	2	2	2	2	2
1174 Security managers	5	1	8.1	9.1	5	5	5	5
1181 Hospital and health service managers	2	1	8.1	9.1	2	2	2	2
1182 Pharmacy managers	5	3.3	3.3	3.3	2	5	5	5
1183 Healthcare practice managers	5	1	8.1	9.1	5	5	5	5
1184 Social services managers	2	1	8.1	9.1	2	2	2	2
1185 Residential and day care managers	5	1	8.1	9.1	5	5	5	5
1211 Farm managers	5	1	8.2	9.2	5	5	5	5
1212 Natural environment and conservation managers	2	1	8.1	9.1	2	5	5	5
1219 Managers in animal husbandry, forestry and fishing n.e.c.	9.2	1	8.2	9.2	5	5	5	5
1221 Hotel and accommodation managers	9.1	1	8.1	9.1	5	5	5	5
1222 Conference and exhibition managers	5	1	8.1	9.1	5	5	5	5
1223 Restaurant and catering managers	8.1	1	8.1	9.1	5	5	5	5
1224 Publicans and managers of licensed premises	5	1	8.1	9.1	5	5	5	5
1225 Leisure and sports managers	5	1	8.1	9.1	5	5	5	5
1226 Travel agency managers	5	1	8.1	9.1	5	5	5	5
1231 Property, housing and land managers	2	1	8.1	9.1	2	5	5	5
1232 Garage managers and proprietors	8.1	1	8.1	9.1	5	5	5	5
1233 Hairdressing and beauty salon managers and proprietors	8.1	1	8.1	9.1	5	5	5	5
1234 Shopkeepers and wholesale/retail dealers	8.1	1	8.1	9.1	5	5	5	5
1235 Recycling and refuse disposal managers	5	1	8.1	9.1	5	5	5	5
1239 Managers and proprietors in other services n.e.c.	5	1	8.1	9.1	5	5	5	5
2111 Chemists	3.1	3.3	3.3	3.3	3.1	3.1	3.1	3.1
2112 Biological scientists and biochemists	3.1	3.3	3.3	3.3	3.1	3.1	3.1	3.1
2113 Physicists, geologists and meteorologists	3.1	3.3	3.3	3.3	3.1	3.1	3.1	3.1

Please note: This derivation table has no empty cells. The shaded cells have been filled using the priority order rules. See Appendix A.

Table 10 - *continued*

Standard Occupational Classification 2000 unit group		Simplified NS-SEC	Employment status/size of organisation						
			1 Employers - large organisations	2 Employers - small organisations	3 Self-employed, no employees	4 Managers - large organisations	5 Managers - small organisations	6 Supervisors	7 Other employees
2121	Civil engineers	3.1	3.3	3.3	3.3	3.1	3.1	3.1	3.1
2122	Mechanical engineers	3.1	3.3	3.3	3.3	3.1	3.1	3.1	3.1
2123	Electrical engineers	3.1	3.3	3.3	3.3	3.1	3.1	3.1	3.1
2124	Electronics engineers	3.1	3.3	3.3	3.3	3.1	3.1	3.1	3.1
2125	Chemical engineers	3.1	3.3	3.3	3.3	3.1	3.1	3.1	3.1
2126	Design and development engineers	3.1	3.3	3.3	3.3	3.1	3.1	3.1	3.1
2127	Production and process engineers	4.1	1	4.3	4.3	4.1	4.1	4.1	4.1
2128	Planning and quality control engineers	4.1	1	4.3	4.3	4.1	4.1	4.1	4.1
2129	Engineering professionals n.e.c.	3.1	3.3	3.3	3.3	3.1	3.1	3.1	3.1
2131	IT strategy and planning professionals	3.2	3.4	3.4	3.4	3.2	3.2	3.2	3.2
2132	Software professionals	3.2	3.4	3.4	3.4	3.2	3.2	3.2	3.2
2211	Medical practitioners	3.1	3.3	3.3	3.3	3.1	3.1	3.1	3.1
2212	Psychologists	3.1	3.3	3.3	3.3	3.1	3.1	3.1	3.1
2213	Pharmacists/pharmacologists	3.1	3.3	3.3	3.3	3.1	3.1	3.1	3.1
2214	Ophthalmic opticians	4.1	1	4.3	4.3	4.1	4.1	4.1	4.1
2215	Dental practitioners	3.3	3.3	3.3	3.3	3.1	3.1	3.1	3.1
2216	Veterinarians	3.1	3.3	3.3	3.3	3.1	3.1	3.1	3.1
2311	Higher education teaching professionals	3.1	3.3	3.3	3.3	3.1	3.1	3.1	3.1
2312	Further education teaching professionals	4.1	1	4.3	4.3	4.1	4.1	4.1	4.1
2313	Education officers, school inspectors	3.1	3.1	3.1	3.1	3.1	3.1	3.1	3.1
2314	Secondary education teaching professionals	4.1	1	4.3	4.3	4.1	4.1	4.1	4.1
2315	Primary and nursery education teaching professionals	4.1	1	4.3	4.3	4.1	4.1	4.1	4.1
2316	Special needs education teaching professionals	4.1	1	4.3	4.3	4.1	4.1	4.1	4.1
2317	Registrars and senior administrators of educational establishments	3.1	3.1	3.1	3.1	3.1	3.1	3.1	3.1
2319	Teaching professionals n.e.c.	9.1	1	8.1	9.1	7.3	7.3	6	7.3
2321	Scientific researchers	3.1	3.3	3.3	3.3	3.1	3.1	3.1	3.1
2322	Social science researchers	3.1	3.3	3.3	3.3	3.1	3.1	3.1	3.1
2329	Researchers n.e.c.	3.1	3.3	3.3	3.3	3.1	3.1	3.1	3.1
2411	Solicitors and lawyers, judges and coroners	3.1	3.3	3.3	3.3	3.1	3.1	3.1	3.1
2419	Legal professionals n.e.c.	3.1	3.3	3.3	3.3	3.1	3.1	3.1	3.1
2421	Chartered and certified accountants	3.1	3.3	3.3	3.3	3.1	3.1	3.1	3.1
2422	Management accountants	3.2	3.4	3.4	3.4	3.2	3.2	3.2	3.2
2423	Management consultants, actuaries, economists and statisticians	3.1	3.3	3.3	3.3	3.1	3.1	3.1	3.1
2431	Architects	3.1	3.3	3.3	3.3	3.1	3.1	3.1	3.1
2432	Town planners	3.1	3.3	3.3	3.3	3.1	3.1	3.1	3.1
2433	Quantity surveyors	4.1	1	4.3	4.3	4.1	4.1	4.1	4.1
2434	Chartered surveyors (not quantity surveyors)	3.1	3.3	3.3	3.3	3.1	3.1	3.1	3.1
2441	Public service administrative professionals	4.1	4.1	4.1	4.1	4.1	4.1	4.1	4.1
2442	Social workers	4.1	4.3	4.3	4.3	4.1	4.1	4.1	4.1
2443	Probation officers	3.2	3.2	3.2	3.2	3.2	3.2	3.2	3.2
2444	Clergy	3.1	3.3	3.3	3.3	3.1	3.1	3.1	3.1
2451	Librarians	4.1	4.3	4.3	4.3	4.1	4.1	4.1	4.1
2452	Archivists and curators	4.1	4.3	4.3	4.3	4.1	4.1	4.1	4.1
3111	Laboratory technicians	4.1	1	4.3	4.3	4.1	4.1	4.1	4.1
3112	Electrical/electronics technicians	7.3	1	8.1	9.1	7.3	7.3	6	7.3
3113	Engineering technicians	4.1	1	4.3	4.3	4.1	4.1	4.1	4.1
3114	Building and civil engineering technicians	4.1	1	4.3	4.3	4.1	4.1	4.1	4.1
3115	Quality assurance technicians	11.1	1	8.1	9.1	11.1	11.1	10	11.1
3119	Science and engineering technicians n.e.c.	4.1	1	4.3	4.3	4.1	4.1	4.1	4.1
3121	Architectural technologists and town planning technicians	4.1	1	4.3	4.3	4.1	4.1	4.1	4.1
3122	Draughtspersons	7.3	1	8.1	9.1	7.3	7.3	6	7.3
3123	Building inspectors	4.1	4.3	4.3	4.3	4.1	4.1	4.1	4.1
3131	IT operations technicians	4.1	1	4.3	4.3	4.1	4.1	4.1	4.1
3132	IT user support technicians	4.1	1	4.3	4.3	4.1	4.1	4.1	4.1
3211	Nurses	4.1	1	4.3	4.3	4.1	4.1	4.1	4.1
3212	Midwives	4.1	1	4.3	4.3	4.1	4.1	4.1	4.1
3213	Paramedics	6	6	6	7.2	7.2	7.2	6	7.2
3214	Medical radiographers	4.1	1	4.3	4.3	4.1	4.1	4.1	4.1
3215	Chiropodists	4.1	1	4.3	4.3	4.1	4.1	4.1	4.1
3216	Dispensing opticians	7.3	1	8.1	9.1	7.3	7.3	6	7.3

Please note: This derivation table has no empty cells. The shaded cells have been filled using the priority order rules. See Appendix A.

Table 10 - *continued*

Standard Occupational Classification 2000 unit group	Simplified NS-SEC	Employment status/size of organisation						
		1 Employers - large organisations	2 Employers - small organisations	3 Self-employed, no employees	4 Managers - large organisations	5 Managers - small organisations	6 Supervisors	7 Other employees
3217 Pharmaceutical dispensers	12.1	1	8.1	9.1	12.1	12.1	10	12.1
3218 Medical and dental technicians	7.3	1	8.1	9.1	7.3	7.3	6	7.3
3221 Physiotherapists	4.1	1	4.3	4.3	4.1	4.1	4.1	4.1
3222 Occupational therapists	4.1	1	4.3	4.3	4.1	4.1	4.1	4.1
3223 Speech and language therapists	3.2	3.4	3.4	3.4	3.2	3.2	3.2	3.2
3229 Therapists n.e.c.	4.3	1	4.3	4.3	4.1	4.1	4.1	4.1
3231 Youth and community workers	4.1	1	4.3	4.3	4.1	4.1	4.1	4.1
3232 Housing and welfare officers	4.1	1	4.3	4.3	4.1	4.1	4.1	4.1
3311 NCOs and other ranks	7.2	6	6	7.2	7.2	7.2	6	7.2
3312 Police officers (sergeant and below)	7.2	6	6	7.2	7.2	7.2	6	7.2
3313 Fire service officers (leading fire officer and below)	7.2	6	6	7.2	7.2	7.2	6	7.2
3314 Prison service officers (below principal officer)	7.2	6	6	7.2	7.2	7.2	6	7.2
3319 Protective service associate professionals n.e.c.	4.1	4.1	4.1	4.1	4.1	4.1	4.1	4.1
3411 Artists	4.3	1	4.3	4.3	4.1	4.1	4.1	4.1
3412 Authors, writers	4.3	1	4.3	4.3	4.1	4.1	4.1	4.1
3413 Actors, entertainers	4.3	1	4.3	4.3	4.1	4.1	4.1	4.1
3414 Dancers and choreographers	4.3	1	4.3	4.3	4.1	4.1	4.1	4.1
3415 Musicians	4.3	1	4.3	4.3	4.1	4.1	4.1	4.1
3416 Arts officers, producers and directors	4.3	1	4.3	4.3	4.1	4.1	4.1	4.1
3421 Graphic designers	7.3	1	8.1	9.1	7.3	7.3	6	7.3
3422 Product, clothing and related designers	9.1	1	8.1	9.1	7.3	7.3	6	7.3
3431 Journalists, newspaper and periodical editors	4.1	1	4.3	4.3	4.1	4.1	4.1	4.1
3432 Broadcasting associate professionals	4.1	1	4.3	4.3	4.1	4.1	4.1	4.1
3433 Public relations officers	4.1	1	4.3	4.3	4.1	4.1	4.1	4.1
3434 Photographers and audio-visual equipment operators	7.2	1	8.1	9.1	7.2	7.2	6	7.2
3441 Sports players	4.1	1	4.3	4.3	4.1	4.1	4.1	4.1
3442 Sports coaches, instructors and officials	4.1	1	4.3	4.3	4.1	4.1	4.1	4.1
3443 Fitness instructors	12.2	1	8.1	9.1	12.2	12.2	10	12.2
3449 Sports and fitness occupations n.e.c.	7.2	1	8.1	9.1	7.2	7.2	6	7.2
3511 Air traffic controllers	4.1	4.1	4.1	4.1	4.1	4.1	4.1	4.1
3512 Aircraft pilots and flight engineers	3.2	3.4	3.4	3.4	3.2	3.2	3.2	3.2
3513 Ship and hovercraft officers	4.1	1	4.3	4.3	4.1	4.1	4.1	4.1
3514 Train drivers	11.1	10	10	11.1	11.1	11.1	10	11.1
3520 Legal associate professionals	7.1	1	8.1	9.1	7.1	7.1	6	7.1
3531 Estimators, valuers and assessors	4.1	1	4.3	4.3	4.1	4.1	4.1	4.1
3532 Brokers	3.2	3.4	3.4	3.4	3.2	3.2	3.2	3.2
3533 Insurance underwriters	3.2	3.4	3.4	3.4	3.2	3.2	3.2	3.2
3534 Finance and investment analysts/advisers	4.1	1	4.3	4.3	4.1	4.1	4.1	4.1
3535 Taxation experts	3.2	3.4	3.4	3.4	3.2	3.2	3.2	3.2
3536 Importers, exporters	4.2	1	4.4	4.4	4.2	4.2	4.2	4.2
3537 Financial and accounting technicians	4.2	1	4.4	4.4	4.2	4.2	4.2	4.2
3539 Business and related associate professionals n.e.c.	4.1	1	4.3	4.3	4.1	4.1	4.1	4.1
3541 Buyers and purchasing officers	4.1	1	4.3	4.3	4.1	4.1	4.1	4.1
3542 Sales representatives	4.2	1	4.4	4.4	4.2	4.2	4.2	4.2
3543 Marketing associate professionals	4.1	1	4.3	4.3	4.1	4.1	4.1	4.1
3544 Estate agents, auctioneers	4.1	1	4.3	4.3	4.1	4.1	4.1	4.1
3551 Conservation and environmental protection officers	3.1	3.3	3.3	3.3	3.1	3.1	3.1	3.1
3552 Countryside and park rangers	7.2	1	8.1	9.1	7.2	7.2	6	7.2
3561 Public service associate professionals	4.1	4.1	4.1	4.1	4.1	4.1	4.1	4.1
3562 Personnel and industrial relations officers	4.1	1	4.3	4.3	4.1	4.1	4.1	4.1
3563 Vocational and industrial trainers and instructors	4.1	1	4.3	4.3	4.1	4.1	4.1	4.1
3564 Careers advisers and vocational guidance specialists	4.1	1	4.3	4.3	4.1	4.1	4.1	4.1
3565 Inspectors of factories, utilities and trading standards	4.1	4.1	4.1	4.1	4.1	4.1	4.1	4.1
3566 Statutory examiners	4.1	4.1	4.1	4.1	4.1	4.1	4.1	4.1
|3567 Occupational hygienists and safety officers (health and safety)	4.1	1	4.3	4.3	4.1	4.1	4.1	4.1
3568 Environmental health officers	3.2	3.2	3.2	3.2	3.2	3.2	3.2	3.2
4111 Civil Service executive officers	4.1	4.1	4.1	4.1	4.1	4.1	4.1	4.1
4112 Civil Service administrative officers and assistants	7.1	6	6	7.1	7.1	7.1	6	7.1

Please note: This derivation table has no empty cells. The shaded cells have been filled using the priority order rules. See Appendix A.
| Indicates a change to the original shading. This does not affect the values in the cells.

Table 10 - *continued*

Standard Occupational Classification 2000 unit group		Simplified NS-SEC	Employment status/size of organisation						
			1 Employers - large organisations	2 Employers - small organisations	3 Self-employed, no employees	4 Managers - large organisations	5 Managers - small organisations	6 Supervisors	7 Other employees
4113	Local government clerical officers and assistants	7.1	6	6	7.1	7.1	7.1	6	7.1
4114	Officers of non-governmental organisations	4.1	1	4.3	4.3	4.1	4.1	4.1	4.1
4121	Credit controllers	7.1	1	8.1	9.1	7.1	7.1	6	7.1
4122	Accounts and wages clerks, book-keepers, other financial clerks	7.1	1	8.1	9.1	7.1	7.1	6	7.1
4123	Counter clerks	7.1	1	8.1	9.1	7.1	7.1	6	7.1
4131	Filing and other records assistants/clerks	7.1	1	8.1	9.1	7.1	7.1	6	7.1
4132	Pensions and insurance clerks	7.1	1	8.1	9.1	7.1	7.1	6	7.1
4133	Stock control clerks	12.6	1	8.1	9.1	12.6	12.6	10	12.6
4134	Transport and distribution clerks	7.1	1	8.1	9.1	7.1	7.1	6	7.1
4135	Library assistants/clerks	7.1	1	8.1	9.1	7.1	7.1	6	7.1
4136	Database assistants/clerks	7.1	1	8.1	9.1	7.1	7.1	6	7.1
4137	Market research interviewers	12.6	1	8.1	9.1	12.6	12.6	10	12.6
4141	Telephonists	12.6	1	8.1	9.1	12.6	12.6	10	12.6
4142	Communication operators	11.1	1	8.1	9.1	11.1	11.1	10	11.1
4150	General office assistants/clerks	7.2	1	8.1	9.1	7.2	7.2	6	7.2
4211	Medical secretaries	7.1	1	8.1	9.1	7.1	7.1	6	7.1
4212	Legal secretaries	7.1	1	8.1	9.1	7.1	7.1	6	7.1
4213	School secretaries	7.1	1	8.1	9.1	7.1	7.1	6	7.1
4214	Company secretaries	7.1	1	8.1	9.1	7.1	7.1	6	7.1
4215	Personal assistants and other secretaries	7.1	1	8.1	9.1	7.1	7.1	6	7.1
4216	Receptionists	12.6	1	8.1	9.1	12.6	12.6	10	12.6
4217	Typists	7.1	1	8.1	9.1	7.1	7.1	6	7.1
5111	Farmers	9.2	1	8.2	9.2	6	6	6	6
5112	Horticultural trades	12.5	1	8.2	9.2	12.5	12.5	10	12.5
5113	Gardeners and groundsmen/groundswomen	11.1	1	8.1	9.1	11.1	11.1	10	11.1
5119	Agricultural and fishing trades n.e.c.	9.2	1	8.2	9.2	11.1	11.1	10	11.1
5211	Smiths and forge workers	13.3	1	8.1	9.1	13.3	13.3	10	13.3
5212	Moulders, core makers, die casters	12.3	1	8.1	9.1	12.3	12.3	10	12.3
5213	Sheet metal workers	12.3	1	8.1	9.1	12.3	12.3	10	12.3
5214	Metal plate workers, shipwrights, riveters	13.3	1	8.1	9.1	13.3	13.3	10	13.3
5215	Welding trades	13.3	1	8.1	9.1	13.3	13.3	10	13.3
5216	Pipe fitters	13.3	1	8.1	9.1	13.3	13.3	10	13.3
5221	Metal machining setters and setter-operators	12.3	1	8.1	9.1	12.3	12.3	10	12.3
5222	Tool makers, tool fitters and markers-out	11.1	1	8.1	9.1	11.1	11.1	10	11.1
5223	Metal working production and maintenance fitters	11.1	1	8.1	9.1	11.1	11.1	10	11.1
5224	Precision instrument makers and repairers	11.1	1	8.1	9.1	11.1	11.1	10	11.1
5231	Motor mechanics, auto engineers	11.1	1	8.1	9.1	11.1	11.1	10	11.1
5232	Vehicle body builders and repairers	11.1	1	8.1	9.1	11.1	11.1	10	11.1
5233	Auto electricians	11.1	1	8.1	9.1	11.1	11.1	10	11.1
5234	Vehicle spray painters	12.3	1	8.1	9.1	12.3	12.3	10	12.3
5241	Electricians, electrical fitters	11.1	1	8.1	9.1	11.1	11.1	10	11.1
5242	Telecommunications engineers	7.4	1	8.1	9.1	7.4	7.4	6	7.4
5243	Lines repairers and cable jointers	11.1	1	8.1	9.1	11.1	11.1	10	11.1
5244	TV, video and audio engineers	11.1	1	8.1	9.1	11.1	11.1	10	11.1
5245	Computer engineers, installation and maintenance	7.4	1	8.1	9.1	7.4	7.4	6	7.4
5249	Electrical/electronics engineers n.e.c.	7.4	1	8.1	9.1	7.4	7.4	6	7.4
5311	Steel erectors	12.3	1	8.1	9.1	12.3	12.3	10	12.3
5312	Bricklayers, masons	9.1	1	8.1	9.1	13.3	13.3	10	13.3
5313	Roofers, roof tilers and slaters	9.1	1	8.1	9.1	13.2	13.2	10	13.2
5314	Plumbers, heating and ventilating engineers	11.1	1	8.1	9.1	11.1	11.1	10	11.1
5315	Carpenters and joiners	9.1	1	8.1	9.1	13.3	13.3	10	13.3
5316	Glaziers, window fabricators and fitters	9.1	1	8.1	9.1	13.2	13.2	10	13.2
5319	Construction trades n.e.c.	9.1	1	8.1	9.1	12.4	12.4	10	12.4
5321	Plasterers	9.1	1	8.1	9.1	13.3	13.3	10	13.3
5322	Floorers and wall tilers	9.1	1	8.1	9.1	13.3	13.3	10	13.3
5323	Painters and decorators	9.1	1	8.1	9.1	13.3	13.3	10	13.3
5411	Weavers and knitters	13.3	1	8.1	9.1	13.3	13.3	10	13.3
5412	Upholsterers	13.3	1	8.1	9.1	13.3	13.3	10	13.3
5413	Leather and related trades	13.3	1	8.1	9.1	13.3	13.3	10	13.3
5414	Tailors and dressmakers	12.3	1	8.1	9.1	12.3	12.3	10	12.3

Please note: This derivation table has no empty cells. The shaded cells have been filled using the priority order rules. See Appendix A.
| *Indicates a change to the original shading. This does not affect the values in the cells.*

Table 10 - *continued*

Standard Occupational Classification 2000 unit group	Simplified NS-SEC	Employment status/size of organisation						
		1 Employers - large organisations	2 Employers - small organisations	3 Self-employed, no employees	4 Managers - large organisations	5 Managers - small organisations	6 Supervisors	7 Other employees
5419 Textiles, garments and related trades n.e.c.	13.3	1	8.1	9.1	13.3	13.3	10	13.3
5421 Originators, compositors and print preparers	11.1	1	8.1	9.1	11.1	11.1	10	11.1
5422 Printers	11.1	1	8.1	9.1	11.1	11.1	10	11.1
5423 Bookbinders and print finishers	13.3	1	8.1	9.1	13.3	13.3	10	13.3
5424 Screen printers	11.1	1	8.1	9.1	11.1	11.1	10	11.1
5431 Butchers, meat cutters	13.3	1	8.1	9.1	13.3	13.3	10	13.3
5432 Bakers, flour confectioners	11.1	1	8.1	9.1	11.1	11.1	10	11.1
5433 Fishmongers, poultry dressers	13.3	1	8.1	9.1	13.3	13.3	10	13.3
5434 Chefs, cooks	12.2	1	8.1	9.1	12.2	12.2	10	12.2
5491 Glass and ceramics makers, decorators and finishers	13.3	1	8.1	9.1	13.3	13.3	10	13.3
5492 Furniture makers, other craft woodworkers	13.3	1	8.1	9.1	13.3	13.3	10	13.3
5493 Pattern makers (moulds)	11.1	1	8.1	9.1	11.1	11.1	10	11.1
5494 Musical instrument makers and tuners	9.1	1	8.1	9.1	11.1	11.1	10	11.1
5495 Goldsmiths, silversmiths, precious stone workers	11.1	1	8.1	9.1	11.1	11.1	10	11.1
5496 Floral arrangers, florists	13.1	1	8.1	9.1	13.1	13.1	10	13.1
5499 Hand craft occupations n.e.c.	11.1	1	8.1	9.1	11.1	11.1	10	11.1
6111 Nursing auxiliaries and assistants	7.3	1	8.1	9.1	7.3	7.3	6	7.3
6112 Ambulance staff (excluding paramedics)	7.2	6	6	7.2	7.2	7.2	6	7.2
6113 Dental nurses	12.2	1	8.1	9.1	12.2	12.2	10	12.2
6114 Houseparents and residential wardens	12.7	1	8.1	9.1	12.7	12.7	10	12.7
6115 Care assistants and home carers	12.2	1	8.1	9.1	12.2	12.2	10	12.2
6121 Nursery nurses	7.2	1	8.1	9.1	7.2	7.2	6	7.2
6122 Childminders and related occupations	9.1	1	8.1	9.1	13.1	13.1	10	13.1
6123 Playgroup leaders/assistants	12.7	1	8.1	9.1	12.7	12.7	10	12.7
6124 Educational assistants	12.7	1	8.1	9.1	12.7	12.7	10	12.7
6131 Veterinary nurses and assistants	12.2	1	8.1	9.1	12.2	12.2	10	12.2
6139 Animal care occupations n.e.c.	13.5	1	8.2	9.2	13.5	13.5	10	13.5
6211 Sports and leisure assistants	12.2	1	8.1	9.1	12.2	12.2	10	12.2
6212 Travel agents	7.2	1	8.1	9.1	7.2	7.2	6	7.2
6213 Travel and tour guides	13.1	1	8.1	9.1	13.1	13.1	10	13.1
6214 Air travel assistants	7.2	1	8.1	9.1	7.2	7.2	6	7.2
6215 Rail travel assistants	7.2	1	8.1	9.1	7.2	7.2	6	7.2
6219 Leisure and travel service occupations n.e.c.	13.3	1	8.1	9.1	13.3	13.3	10	13.3
6221 Hairdressers, barbers	13.1	1	8.1	9.1	13.1	13.1	10	13.1
6222 Beauticians and related occupations	9.1	1	8.1	9.1	12.2	12.2	10	12.2
6231 Housekeepers and related occupations	12.2	1	8.1	9.1	12.2	12.2	10	12.2
6232 Caretakers	12.2	1	8.1	9.1	12.2	12.2	10	12.2
6291 Undertakers and mortuary assistants	12.2	1	8.1	9.1	12.2	12.2	10	12.2
6292 Pest control officers	12.2	1	8.1	9.1	12.2	12.2	10	12.2
7111 Sales and retail assistants	12.1	1	8.1	9.1	12.1	12.1	10	12.1
7112 Retail cashiers and check-out operators	12.1	1	8.1	9.1	12.1	12.1	10	12.1
7113 Telephone salespersons	12.1	1	8.1	9.1	12.1	12.1	10	12.1
7121 Collector salespersons and credit agents	12.1	1	8.1	9.1	12.1	12.1	10	12.1
7122 Debt, rent and other cash collectors	7.2	1	8.1	9.1	7.2	7.2	6	7.2
7123 Roundsmen/women and van salespersons	13.3	1	8.1	9.1	13.3	13.3	10	13.3
7124 Market and street traders and assistants	9.1	1	8.1	9.1	13.1	13.1	10	13.1
7125 Merchandisers and window dressers	7.2	1	8.1	9.1	7.2	7.2	6	7.2
7129 Sales related occupations n.e.c.	7.2	1	8.1	9.1	7.2	7.2	6	7.2
7211 Call centre agents/operators	7.2	1	8.1	9.1	7.2	7.2	6	7.2
7212 Customer care occupations	7.2	1	8.1	9.1	7.2	7.2	6	7.2
8111 Food, drink and tobacco process operatives	12.4	1	8.1	9.1	12.4	12.4	10	12.4
8112 Glass and ceramics process operatives	12.3	1	8.1	9.1	12.3	12.3	10	12.3
8113 Textile process operatives	13.2	1	8.1	9.1	13.2	13.2	10	13.2
8114 Chemical and related process operatives	11.2	1	8.1	9.1	11.2	11.2	10	11.2
8115 Rubber process operatives	12.3	1	8.1	9.1	12.3	12.3	10	12.3
8116 Plastics process operatives	12.4	1	8.1	9.1	12.4	12.4	10	12.4
8117 Metal making and treating process operatives	12.3	1	8.1	9.1	12.3	12.3	10	12.3
8118 Electroplaters	12.3	1	8.1	9.1	12.3	12.3	10	12.3

Please note: This derivation table has no empty cells. The shaded cells have been filled using the priority order rules. See Appendix A.

Table 10 - *continued*

Standard Occupational Classification 2000 unit group	Simplified NS-SEC	Employment status/size of organisation						
		1 Employers - large organisations	2 Employers - small organisations	3 Self-employed, no employees	4 Managers - large organisations	5 Managers - small organisations	6 Supervisors	7 Other employees
8119 Process operatives n.e.c.	12.4	1	8.1	9.1	12.4	12.4	10	12.4
8121 Paper and wood machine operatives	12.3	1	8.1	9.1	12.3	12.3	10	12.3
8122 Coal mine operatives	13.3	1	8.1	9.1	13.3	13.3	10	13.3
8123 Quarry workers and related operatives	11.2	1	8.1	9.1	11.2	11.2	10	11.2
8124 Energy plant operatives	12.4	1	8.1	9.1	12.4	12.4	10	12.4
8125 Metal working machine operatives	12.4	1	8.1	9.1	12.4	12.4	10	12.4
8126 Water and sewerage plant operatives	11.2	1	8.1	9.1	11.2	11.2	10	11.2
8129 Plant and machine operatives n.e.c.	12.4	1	8.1	9.1	12.4	12.4	10	12.4
8131 Assemblers (electrical products)	12.4	1	8.1	9.1	12.4	12.4	10	12.4
8132 Assemblers (vehicles and metal goods)	12.4	1	8.1	9.1	12.4	12.4	10	12.4
8133 Routine inspectors and testers	11.2	1	8.1	9.1	11.2	11.2	10	11.2
8134 Weighers, graders, sorters	13.2	1	8.1	9.1	13.2	13.2	10	13.2
8135 Tyre, exhaust and windscreen fitters	12.4	1	8.1	9.1	12.4	12.4	10	12.4
8136 Clothing cutters	12.3	1	8.1	9.1	12.3	12.3	10	12.3
8137 Sewing machinists	13.2	1	8.1	9.1	13.2	13.2	10	13.2
8138 Routine laboratory testers	7.3	1	8.1	9.1	7.3	7.3	6	7.3
8139 Assemblers and routine operatives n.e.c.	13.2	1	8.1	9.1	13.2	13.2	10	13.2
8141 Scaffolders, stagers, riggers	12.4	1	8.1	9.1	12.4	12.4	10	12.4
8142 Road construction operatives	10	1	8.1	9.1	12.4	12.4	10	12.4
8143 Rail construction and maintenance operatives	11.2	1	8.1	9.1	11.2	11.2	10	11.2
8149 Construction operatives n.e.c.	10	1	8.1	9.1	13.4	13.4	10	13.4
8211 Heavy goods vehicle drivers	13.3	1	8.1	9.1	13.3	13.3	10	13.3
8212 Van drivers	13.3	1	8.1	9.1	13.3	13.3	10	13.3
8213 Bus and coach drivers	13.3	1	8.1	9.1	13.3	13.3	10	13.3
8214 Taxi, cab drivers and chauffeurs	9.1	1	8.1	9.1	13.3	13.3	10	13.3
8215 Driving instructors	9.1	1	8.1	9.1	12.2	12.2	10	12.2
8216 Rail transport operatives	11.2	1	8.1	9.1	11.2	11.2	10	11.2
8217 Seafarers (merchant navy); barge, lighter and boat operatives	12.4	1	8.1	9.1	12.4	12.4	10	12.4
8218 Air transport operatives	11.2	1	8.1	9.1	11.2	11.2	10	11.2
8219 Transport operatives n.e.c.	10	1	8.1	9.1	11.2	11.2	10	11.2
8221 Crane drivers	12.3	1	8.1	9.1	12.3	12.3	10	12.3
8222 Fork-lift truck drivers	12.3	1	8.1	9.1	12.3	12.3	10	12.3
8223 Agricultural machinery drivers	12.5	1	8.2	9.2	12.5	12.5	10	12.5
8229 Mobile machine drivers and operatives n.e.c.	13.3	1	8.1	9.1	13.3	13.3	10	13.3
9111 Farm workers	12.5	1	8.2	9.2	12.5	12.5	10	12.5
9112 Forestry workers	9.2	1	8.2	9.2	12.5	12.5	10	12.5
9119 Fishing and agriculture related occupations n.e.c.	13.5	1	8.2	9.2	13.5	13.5	10	13.5
9121 Labourers in building and woodworking trades	13.4	1	8.1	9.1	13.4	13.4	10	13.4
9129 Labourers in other construction trades n.e.c.	13.4	1	8.1	9.1	13.4	13.4	10	13.4
9131 Labourers in foundries	13.4	1	8.1	9.1	13.4	13.4	10	13.4
9132 Industrial cleaning process occupations	13.4	1	8.1	9.1	13.4	13.4	10	13.4
9133 Printing machine minders and assistants	12.3	1	8.1	9.1	12.3	12.3	10	12.3
9134 Packers, bottlers, canners, fillers	13.2	1	8.1	9.1	13.2	13.2	10	13.2
9139 Labourers in process and plant operations n.e.c.	13.4	1	8.1	9.1	13.4	13.4	10	13.4
9141 Stevedores, dockers and slingers	13.4	1	8.1	9.1	13.4	13.4	10	13.4
9149 Other goods handling and storage occupations n.e.c.	13.4	1	8.1	9.1	13.4	13.4	10	13.4
9211 Postal workers, mail sorters, messengers, couriers	12.2	1	8.1	9.1	12.2	12.2	10	12.2
9219 Elementary office occupations n.e.c.	12.6	1	8.1	9.1	12.6	12.6	10	12.6
9221 Hospital porters	12.2	1	8.1	9.1	12.2	12.2	10	12.2
9222 Hotel porters	13.1	1	8.1	9.1	13.1	13.1	10	13.1
9223 Kitchen and catering assistants	12.2	1	8.1	9.1	12.2	12.2	10	12.2
9224 Waiters, waitresses	13.1	1	8.1	9.1	13.1	13.1	10	13.1
9225 Bar staff	13.1	1	8.1	9.1	13.1	13.1	10	13.1
9226 Leisure and theme park attendants	13.1	1	8.1	9.1	13.1	13.1	10	13.1
9229 Elementary personal services occupations n.e.c.	13.1	1	8.1	9.1	13.1	13.1	10	13.1
9231 Window cleaners	9.1	1	8.1	9.1	13.2	13.2	10	13.2
9232 Road sweepers	13.4	1	8.1	9.1	13.4	13.4	10	13.4
9233 Cleaners, domestics	13.4	1	8.1	9.1	13.4	13.4	10	13.4
9234 Launderers, dry cleaners, pressers	13.2	1	8.1	9.1	13.2	13.2	10	13.2
9235 Refuse and salvage occupations	13.4	1	8.1	9.1	13.4	13.4	10	13.4

Please note: This derivation table has no empty cells. The shaded cells have been filled using the priority order rules. See Appendix A.

Table 10 - *continued*

Standard Occupational Classification 2000 unit group	Simplified NS-SEC	Employment status/size of organisation						
		1 Employers - large organisations	2 Employers - small organisations	3 Self-employed, no employees	4 Managers - large organisations	5 Managers - small organisations	6 Supervisors	7 Other employees
9239 Elementary cleaning occupations n.e.c.	13.4	1	8.1	9.1	13.4	13.4	10	13.4
9241 Security guards and related occupations	12.2	1	8.1	9.1	12.2	12.2	10	12.2
9242 Traffic wardens	12.2	10	10	12.2	12.2	12.2	10	12.2
9243 School crossing patrol attendants	13.1	10	10	13.1	13.1	13.1	10	13.1
9244 School mid-day assistants	13.1	10	10	13.1	13.1	13.1	10	13.1
9245 Car park attendants	13.4	1	8.1	9.1	13.4	13.4	10	13.4
9249 Elementary security occupations n.e.c.	12.2	1	8.1	9.1	12.2	12.2	10	12.2
9251 Shelf fillers	12.1	1	8.1	9.1	12.1	12.1	10	12.1
9259 Elementary sales occupations n.e.c.	12.1	1	8.1	9.1	12.1	12.1	10	12.1

Please note: This derivation table has no empty cells. The shaded cells have been filled using the priority order rules. See Appendix A.

Table 11

NS-SEC based on SOC2000 simplified and full derivation table: analytic classes

Standard Occupational Classification 2000 unit group	Simplified NS-SEC	Employment status/size of organisation						
		1 Employers - large organisations	2 Employers - small organisations	3 Self-employed, no employees	4 Managers - large organisations	5 Managers - small organisations	6 Supervisors	7 Other employees
1111 Senior officials in national government	1.1	1.1	1.1	1.1	1.1	1.1	1.1	1.1
1112 Directors and chief executives of major organisations	1.1	1.1	1.1	1.1	1.1	1.1	1.1	1.1
1113 Senior officials in local government	1.1	4	4	4	1.1	1.1	1.1	1.1
1114 Senior officials of special interest organisations	2	1.1	4	4	1.1	2	2	2
1121 Production, works and maintenance managers	1.1	1.1	4	4	1.1	2	2	2
1122 Managers in construction	2	1.1	4	4	2	2	2	2
1123 Managers in mining and energy	1.1	1.1	4	4	1.1	2	2	2
1131 Financial managers and chartered secretaries	1.1	1.2	1.2	1.2	1.1	1.1	1.1	1.1
1132 Marketing and sales managers	1.1	1.1	4	4	1.1	2	2	2
1133 Purchasing managers	1.1	1.1	4	4	1.1	2	2	2
1134 Advertising and public relations managers	1.1	1.1	4	4	1.1	2	2	2
1135 Personnel, training and industrial relations managers	1.1	1.1	4	4	1.1	2	2	2
1136 Information and communication technology managers	1.1	1.1	4	4	1.1	2	2	2
1137 Research and development managers	1.1	1.2	1.2	1.2	1.1	2	2	2
1141 Quality assurance managers	2	1.1	4	4	2	2	2	2
1142 Customer care managers	2	1.1	4	4	2	2	2	2
1151 Financial institution managers	2	1.1	4	4	2	2	2	2
1152 Office managers	2	1.1	4	4	2	2	2	2
1161 Transport and distribution managers	2	1.1	4	4	2	2	2	2
1162 Storage and warehouse managers	2	1.1	4	4	2	2	2	2
1163 Retail and wholesale managers	2	1.1	4	4	2	2	2	2
1171 Officers in armed forces	1.1	1.1	1.1	1.1	1.1	1.1	1.1	1.1
1172 Police officers (inspectors and above)	1.1	1.1	1.1	1.1	1.1	1.1	1.1	1.1
1173 Senior officers in fire, ambulance, prison and related services	1.1	1.1	1.1	1.1	1.1	1.1	1.1	1.1
1174 Security managers	2	1.1	4	4	2	2	2	2
1181 Hospital and health service managers	1.1	1.1	4	4	1.1	1.1	1.1	1.1
1182 Pharmacy managers	2	1.2	1.2	1.2	1.1	2	2	2
1183 Healthcare practice managers	2	1.1	4	4	2	2	2	2
1184 Social services managers	1.1	1.1	4	4	1.1	1.1	1.1	1.1
1185 Residential and day care managers	2	1.1	4	4	2	2	2	2
1211 Farm managers	2	1.1	4	4	2	2	2	2
1212 Natural environment and conservation managers	1.1	1.1	4	4	1.1	2	2	2
1219 Managers in animal husbandry, forestry and fishing n.e.c.	4	1.1	4	4	2	2	2	2
1221 Hotel and accommodation managers	4	1.1	4	4	2	2	2	2
1222 Conference and exhibition managers	2	1.1	4	4	2	2	2	2
1223 Restaurant and catering managers	4	1.1	4	4	2	2	2	2
1224 Publicans and managers of licensed premises	2	1.1	4	4	2	2	2	2
1225 Leisure and sports managers	2	1.1	4	4	2	2	2	2
1226 Travel agency managers	2	1.1	4	4	2	2	2	2
1231 Property, housing and land managers	1.1	1.1	4	4	1.1	2	2	2
1232 Garage managers and proprietors	4	1.1	4	4	2	2	2	2
1233 Hairdressing and beauty salon managers and proprietors	4	1.1	4	4	2	2	2	2
1234 Shopkeepers and wholesale/retail dealers	4	1.1	4	4	2	2	2	2
1235 Recycling and refuse disposal managers	2	1.1	4	4	2	2	2	2
1239 Managers and proprietors in other services n.e.c.	2	1.1	4	4	2	2	2	2
2111 Chemists	1.2	1.2	1.2	1.2	1.2	1.2	1.2	1.2
2112 Biological scientists and biochemists	1.2	1.2	1.2	1.2	1.2	1.2	1.2	1.2
2113 Physicists, geologists and meteorologists	1.2	1.2	1.2	1.2	1.2	1.2	1.2	1.2

Please note: This derivation table has no empty cells. The shaded cells have been filled using the priority order rules. See Appendix A.

Table 11 - *continued*

Standard Occupational Classification 2000 unit group		Simplified NS-SEC	Employment status/size of organisation						
			1 Employers - large organisations	2 Employers - small organisations	3 Self-employed, no employees	4 Managers - large organisations	5 Managers - small organisations	6 Supervisors	7 Other employees
2121	Civil engineers	1.2	1.2	1.2	1.2	1.2	1.2	1.2	1.2
2122	Mechanical engineers	1.2	1.2	1.2	1.2	1.2	1.2	1.2	1.2
2123	Electrical engineers	1.2	1.2	1.2	1.2	1.2	1.2	1.2	1.2
2124	Electronics engineers	1.2	1.2	1.2	1.2	1.2	1.2	1.2	1.2
2125	Chemical engineers	1.2	1.2	1.2	1.2	1.2	1.2	1.2	1.2
2126	Design and development engineers	1.2	1.2	1.2	1.2	1.2	1.2	1.2	1.2
2127	Production and process engineers	2	1.1	2	2	2	2	2	2
2128	Planning and quality control engineers	2	1.1	2	2	2	2	2	2
2129	Engineering professionals n.e.c.	1.2	1.2	1.2	1.2	1.2	1.2	1.2	1.2
2131	IT strategy and planning professionals	1.2	1.2	1.2	1.2	1.2	1.2	1.2	1.2
2132	Software professionals	1.2	1.2	1.2	1.2	1.2	1.2	1.2	1.2
2211	Medical practitioners	1.2	1.2	1.2	1.2	1.2	1.2	1.2	1.2
2212	Psychologists	1.2	1.2	1.2	1.2	1.2	1.2	1.2	1.2
2213	Pharmacists/pharmacologists	1.2	1.2	1.2	1.2	1.2	1.2	1.2	1.2
2214	Ophthalmic opticians	2	1.1	2	2	2	2	2	2
2215	Dental practitioners	1.2	1.2	1.2	1.2	1.2	1.2	1.2	1.2
2216	Veterinarians	1.2	1.2	1.2	1.2	1.2	1.2	1.2	1.2
2311	Higher education teaching professionals	1.2	1.2	1.2	1.2	1.2	1.2	1.2	1.2
2312	Further education teaching professionals	2	1.1	2	2	2	2	2	2
2313	Education officers, school inspectors	1.2	1.2	1.2	1.2	1.2	1.2	1.2	1.2
2314	Secondary education teaching professionals	2	1.1	2	2	2	2	2	2
2315	Primary and nursery education teaching professionals	2	1.1	2	2	2	2	2	2
2316	Special needs education teaching professionals	2	1.1	2	2	2	2	2	2
2317	Registrars and senior administrators of educational establishments	1.2	1.2	1.2	1.2	1.2	1.2	1.2	1.2
2319	Teaching professionals n.e.c.	4	1.1	4	4	3	3	2	3
2321	Scientific researchers	1.2	1.2	1.2	1.2	1.2	1.2	1.2	1.2
2322	Social science researchers	1.2	1.2	1.2	1.2	1.2	1.2	1.2	1.2
2329	Researchers n.e.c.	1.2	1.2	1.2	1.2	1.2	1.2	1.2	1.2
2411	Solicitors and lawyers, judges and coroners	1.2	1.2	1.2	1.2	1.2	1.2	1.2	1.2
2419	Legal professionals n.e.c.	1.2	1.2	1.2	1.2	1.2	1.2	1.2	1.2
2421	Chartered and certified accountants	1.2	1.2	1.2	1.2	1.2	1.2	1.2	1.2
2422	Management accountants	1.2	1.2	1.2	1.2	1.2	1.2	1.2	1.2
2423	Management consultants, actuaries, economists and statisticians	1.2	1.2	1.2	1.2	1.2	1.2	1.2	1.2
2431	Architects	1.2	1.2	1.2	1.2	1.2	1.2	1.2	1.2
2432	Town planners	1.2	1.2	1.2	1.2	1.2	1.2	1.2	1.2
2433	Quantity surveyors	2	1.1	2	2	2	2	2	2
2434	Chartered surveyors (not quantity surveyors)	1.2	1.2	1.2	1.2	1.2	1.2	1.2	1.2
2441	Public service administrative professionals	2	2	2	2	2	2	2	2
2442	Social workers	2	2	2	2	2	2	2	2
2443	Probation officers	1.2	1.2	1.2	1.2	1.2	1.2	1.2	1.2
2444	Clergy	1.2	1.2	1.2	1.2	1.2	1.2	1.2	1.2
2451	Librarians	2	2	2	2	2	2	2	2
2452	Archivists and curators	2	2	2	2	2	2	2	2
3111	Laboratory technicians	2	1.1	2	2	2	2	2	2
3112	Electrical/electronics technicians	3	1.1	4	4	3	3	2	3
3113	Engineering technicians	2	1.1	2	2	2	2	2	2
3114	Building and civil engineering technicians	2	1.1	2	2	2	2	2	2
3115	Quality assurance technicians	5	1.1	4	4	5	5	5	5
3119	Science and engineering technicians n.e.c.	2	1.1	2	2	2	2	2	2
3121	Architectural technologists and town planning technicians	2	1.1	2	2	2	2	2	2
3122	Draughtspersons	3	1.1	4	4	3	3	2	3
3123	Building inspectors	2	2	2	2	2	2	2	2
3131	IT operations technicians	2	1.1	2	2	2	2	2	2
3132	IT user support technicians	2	1.1	2	2	2	2	2	2
3211	Nurses	2	1.1	2	2	2	2	2	2
3212	Midwives	2	1.1	2	2	2	2	2	2
3213	Paramedics	2	2	2	3	3	3	2	3
3214	Medical radiographers	2	1.1	2	2	2	2	2	2
3215	Chiropodists	2	1.1	2	2	2	2	2	2
3216	Dispensing opticians	3	1.1	4	4	3	3	2	3

Please note: This derivation table has no empty cells. The shaded cells have been filled using the priority order rules. See Appendix A.

Table 11 - *continued*

Standard Occupational Classification 2000 unit group		Simplified NS-SEC	Employment status/size of organisation						
			1 Employers - large organisations	2 Employers - small organisations	3 Self-employed, no employees	4 Managers - large organisations	5 Managers - small organisations	6 Supervisors	7 Other employees
3217	Pharmaceutical dispensers	6	1.1	4	4	6	6	5	6
3218	Medical and dental technicians	3	1.1	4	4	3	3	2	3
3221	Physiotherapists	2	1.1	2	2	2	2	2	2
3222	Occupational therapists	2	1.1	2	2	2	2	2	2
3223	Speech and language therapists	1.2	1.2	1.2	1.2	1.2	1.2	1.2	1.2
3229	Therapists n.e.c.	2	1.1	2	2	2	2	2	2
3231	Youth and community workers	2	1.1	2	2	2	2	2	2
3232	Housing and welfare officers	2	1.1	2	2	2	2	2	2
3311	NCOs and other ranks	3	2	2	3	3	3	2	3
3312	Police officers (sergeant and below)	3	2	2	3	3	3	2	3
3313	Fire service officers (leading fire officer and below)	3	2	2	3	3	3	2	3
3314	Prison service officers (below principal officer)	3	2	2	3	3	3	2	3
3319	Protective service associate professionals n.e.c.	2	2	2	2	2	2	2	2
3411	Artists	2	1.1	2	2	2	2	2	2
3412	Authors, writers	2	1.1	2	2	2	2	2	2
3413	Actors, entertainers	2	1.1	2	2	2	2	2	2
3414	Dancers and choreographers	2	1.1	2	2	2	2	2	2
3415	Musicians	2	1.1	2	2	2	2	2	2
3416	Arts officers, producers and directors	2	1.1	2	2	2	2	2	2
3421	Graphic designers	3	1.1	4	4	3	3	2	3
3422	Product, clothing and related designers	4	1.1	4	4	3	3	2	3
3431	Journalists, newspaper and periodical editors	2	1.1	2	2	2	2	2	2
3432	Broadcasting associate professionals	2	1.1	2	2	2	2	2	2
3433	Public relations officers	2	1.1	2	2	2	2	2	2
3434	Photographers and audio-visual equipment operators	3	1.1	4	4	3	3	2	3
3441	Sports players	2	1.1	2	2	2	2	2	2
3442	Sports coaches, instructors and officials	2	1.1	2	2	2	2	2	2
3443	Fitness instructors	6	1.1	4	4	6	6	5	6
3449	Sports and fitness occupations n.e.c.	3	1.1	4	4	3	3	2	3
3511	Air traffic controllers	2	2	2	2	2	2	2	2
3512	Aircraft pilots and flight engineers	1.2	1.2	1.2	1.2	1.2	1.2	1.2	1.2
3513	Ship and hovercraft officers	2	1.1	2	2	2	2	2	2
3514	Train drivers	5	5	5	5	5	5	5	5
3520	Legal associate professionals	3	1.1	4	4	3	3	2	3
3531	Estimators, valuers and assessors	2	1.1	2	2	2	2	2	2
3532	Brokers	1.2	1.2	1.2	1.2	1.2	1.2	1.2	1.2
3533	Insurance underwriters	1.2	1.2	1.2	1.2	1.2	1.2	1.2	1.2
3534	Finance and investment analysts/advisers	2	1.1	2	2	2	2	2	2
3535	Taxation experts	1.2	1.2	1.2	1.2	1.2	1.2	1.2	1.2
3536	Importers, exporters	2	1.1	2	2	2	2	2	2
3537	Financial and accounting technicians	2	1.1	2	2	2	2	2	2
3539	Business and related associate professionals n.e.c.	2	1.1	2	2	2	2	2	2
3541	Buyers and purchasing officers	2	1.1	2	2	2	2	2	2
3542	Sales representatives	2	1.1	2	2	2	2	2	2
3543	Marketing associate professionals	2	1.1	2	2	2	2	2	2
3544	Estate agents, auctioneers	2	1.1	2	2	2	2	2	2
3551	Conservation and environmental protection officers	1.2	1.2	1.2	1.2	1.2	1.2	1.2	1.2
3552	Countryside and park rangers	3	1.1	4	4	3	3	2	3
3561	Public service associate professionals	2	2	2	2	2	2	2	2
3562	Personnel and industrial relations officers	2	1.1	2	2	2	2	2	2
3563	Vocational and industrial trainers and instructors	2	1.1	2	2	2	2	2	2
3564	Careers advisers and vocational guidance specialists	2	1.1	2	2	2	2	2	2
3565	Inspectors of factories, utilities and trading standards	2	2	2	2	2	2	2	2
3566	Statutory examiners	2	2	2	2	2	2	2	2
3567	Occupational hygienists and safety officers (health and safety)	2	1.1	2	2	2	2	2	2
3568	Environmental health officers	1.2	1.2	1.2	1.2	1.2	1.2	1.2	1.2
4111	Civil Service executive officers	2	2	2	2	2	2	2	2
4112	Civil Service administrative officers and assistants	3	2	2	3	3	3	2	3

Please note: This derivation table has no empty cells. The shaded cells have been filled using the priority order rules. See Appendix A.

Table 11 - *continued*

Standard Occupational Classification 2000 unit group	Simplified NS-SEC	Employment status/size of organisation						
		1 Employers - large organisations	2 Employers - small organisations	3 Self-employed, no employees	4 Managers - large organisations	5 Managers - small organisations	6 Supervisors	7 Other employees
4113 Local government clerical officers and assistants	3	2	2	3	3	3	2	3
4114 Officers of non-governmental organisations	2	1.1	2	2	2	2	2	2
4121 Credit controllers	3	1.1	4	4	3	3	2	3
4122 Accounts and wages clerks, book-keepers, other financial clerks	3	1.1	4	4	3	3	2	3
4123 Counter clerks	3	1.1	4	4	3	3	2	3
4131 Filing and other records assistants/clerks	3	1.1	4	4	3	3	2	3
4132 Pensions and insurance clerks	3	1.1	4	4	3	3	2	3
4133 Stock control clerks	6	1.1	4	4	6	6	5	6
4134 Transport and distribution clerks	3	1.1	4	4	3	3	2	3
4135 Library assistants/clerks	3	1.1	4	4	3	3	2	3
4136 Database assistants/clerks	3	1.1	4	4	3	3	2	3
4137 Market research interviewers	6	1.1	4	4	6	6	5	6
4141 Telephonists	6	1.1	4	4	6	6	5	6
4142 Communication operators	5	1.1	4	4	5	5	5	5
4150 General office assistants/clerks	3	1.1	4	4	3	3	2	3
4211 Medical secretaries	3	1.1	4	4	3	3	2	3
4212 Legal secretaries	3	1.1	4	4	3	3	2	3
4213 School secretaries	3	1.1	4	4	3	3	2	3
4214 Company secretaries	3	1.1	4	4	3	3	2	3
4215 Personal assistants and other secretaries	3	1.1	4	4	3	3	2	3
4216 Receptionists	6	1.1	4	4	6	6	5	6
4217 Typists	3	1.1	4	4	3	3	2	3
5111 Farmers	4	1.1	4	4	2	2	2	2
5112 Horticultural trades	6	1.1	4	4	6	6	5	6
5113 Gardeners and groundsmen/groundswomen	5	1.1	4	4	5	5	5	5
5119 Agricultural and fishing trades n.e.c.	4	1.1	4	4	5	5	5	5
5211 Smiths and forge workers	7	1.1	4	4	7	7	5	7
5212 Moulders, core makers, die casters	6	1.1	4	4	6	6	5	6
5213 Sheet metal workers	6	1.1	4	4	6	6	5	6
5214 Metal plate workers, shipwrights, riveters	7	1.1	4	4	7	7	5	7
5215 Welding trades	7	1.1	4	4	7	7	5	7
5216 Pipe fitters	7	1.1	4	4	7	7	5	7
5221 Metal machining setters and setter-operators	6	1.1	4	4	6	6	5	6
5222 Tool makers, tool fitters and markers-out	5	1.1	4	4	5	5	5	5
5223 Metal working production and maintenance fitters	5	1.1	4	4	5	5	5	5
5224 Precision instrument makers and repairers	5	1.1	4	4	5	5	5	5
5231 Motor mechanics, auto engineers	5	1.1	4	4	5	5	5	5
5232 Vehicle body builders and repairers	5	1.1	4	4	5	5	5	5
5233 Auto electricians	5	1.1	4	4	5	5	5	5
5234 Vehicle spray painters	6	1.1	4	4	6	6	5	6
5241 Electricians, electrical fitters	5	1.1	4	4	5	5	5	5
5242 Telecommunications engineers	3	1.1	4	4	3	3	2	3
5243 Lines repairers and cable joiners	5	1.1	4	4	5	5	5	5
5244 TV, video and audio engineers	5	1.1	4	4	5	5	5	5
5245 Computer engineers, installation and maintenance	3	1.1	4	4	3	3	2	3
5249 Electrical/electronics engineers n.e.c.	3	1.1	4	4	3	3	2	3
5311 Steel erectors	6	1.1	4	4	6	6	5	6
5312 Bricklayers, masons	4	1.1	4	4	7	7	5	7
5313 Roofers, roof tilers and slaters	4	1.1	4	4	7	7	5	7
5314 Plumbers, heating and ventilating engineers	5	1.1	4	4	5	5	5	5
5315 Carpenters and joiners	4	1.1	4	4	7	7	5	7
5316 Glaziers, window fabricators and fitters	4	1.1	4	4	7	7	5	7
5319 Construction trades n.e.c.	4	1.1	4	4	6	6	5	6
5321 Plasterers	4	1.1	4	4	7	7	5	7
5322 Floorers and wall tilers	4	1.1	4	4	7	7	5	7
5323 Painters and decorators	4	1.1	4	4	7	7	5	7
5411 Weavers and knitters	7	1.1	4	4	7	7	5	7
5412 Upholsterers	7	1.1	4	4	7	7	5	7
5413 Leather and related trades	7	1.1	4	4	7	7	5	7
5414 Tailors and dressmakers	6	1.1	4	4	6	6	5	6

Please note: This derivation table has no empty cells. The shaded cells have been filled using the priority order rules. See Appendix A.

Table 11 - *continued*

Standard Occupational Classification 2000 unit group	Simplified NS-SEC	Employment status/size of organisation						
		1 Employers - large organisations	2 Employers - small organisations	3 Self-employed, no employees	4 Managers - large organisations	5 Managers - small organisations	6 Supervisors	7 Other employees
5419 Textiles, garments and related trades n.e.c.	7	1.1	4	4	7	7	5	7
5421 Originators, compositors and print preparers	5	1.1	4	4	5	5	5	5
5422 Printers	5	1.1	4	4	5	5	5	5
5423 Bookbinders and print finishers	7	1.1	4	4	7	7	5	7
5424 Screen printers	5	1.1	4	4	5	5	5	5
5431 Butchers, meat cutters	7	1.1	4	4	7	7	5	7
5432 Bakers, flour confectioners	5	1.1	4	4	5	5	5	5
5433 Fishmongers, poultry dressers	7	1.1	4	4	7	7	5	7
5434 Chefs, cooks	6	1.1	4	4	6	6	5	6
5491 Glass and ceramics makers, decorators and finishers	7	1.1	4	4	7	7	5	7
5492 Furniture makers, other craft woodworkers	7	1.1	4	4	7	7	5	7
5493 Pattern makers (moulds)	5	1.1	4	4	5	5	5	5
5494 Musical instrument makers and tuners	4	1.1	4	4	5	5	5	5
5495 Goldsmiths, silversmiths, precious stone workers	5	1.1	4	4	5	5	5	5
5496 Floral arrangers, florists	7	1.1	4	4	7	7	5	7
5499 Hand craft occupations n.e.c.	5	1.1	4	4	5	5	5	5
6111 Nursing auxiliaries and assistants	3	1.1	4	4	3	3	2	3
6112 Ambulance staff (excluding paramedics)	3	2	2	3	3	3	2	3
6113 Dental nurses	6	1.1	4	4	6	6	5	6
6114 Houseparents and residential wardens	6	1.1	4	4	6	6	5	6
6115 Care assistants and home carers	6	1.1	4	4	6	6	5	6
6121 Nursery nurses	3	1.1	4	4	3	3	2	3
6122 Childminders and related occupations	4	1.1	4	4	7	7	5	7
6123 Playgroup leaders/assistants	6	1.1	4	4	6	6	5	6
6124 Educational assistants	6	1.1	4	4	6	6	5	6
6131 Veterinary nurses and assistants	6	1.1	4	4	6	6	5	6
6139 Animal care occupations n.e.c.	7	1.1	4	4	7	7	5	7
6211 Sports and leisure assistants	6	1.1	4	4	6	6	5	6
6212 Travel agents	3	1.1	4	4	3	3	2	3
6213 Travel and tour guides	7	1.1	4	4	7	7	5	7
6214 Air travel assistants	3	1.1	4	4	3	3	2	3
6215 Rail travel assistants	3	1.1	4	4	3	3	2	3
6219 Leisure and travel service occupations n.e.c.	7	1.1	4	4	7	7	5	7
6221 Hairdressers, barbers	7	1.1	4	4	7	7	5	7
6222 Beauticians and related occupations	4	1.1	4	4	6	6	5	6
6231 Housekeepers and related occupations	6	1.1	4	4	6	6	5	6
6232 Caretakers	6	1.1	4	4	6	6	5	6
6291 Undertakers and mortuary assistants	6	1.1	4	4	6	6	5	6
6292 Pest control officers	6	1.1	4	4	6	6	5	6
7111 Sales and retail assistants	6	1.1	4	4	6	6	5	6
7112 Retail cashiers and check-out operators	6	1.1	4	4	6	6	5	6
7113 Telephone salespersons	6	1.1	4	4	6	6	5	6
7121 Collector salespersons and credit agents	6	1.1	4	4	6	6	5	6
7122 Debt, rent and other cash collectors	3	1.1	4	4	3	3	2	3
7123 Roundsmen/women and van salespersons	7	1.1	4	4	7	7	5	7
7124 Market and street traders and assistants	4	1.1	4	4	7	7	5	7
7125 Merchandisers and window dressers	3	1.1	4	4	3	3	2	3
7129 Sales related occupations n.e.c.	3	1.1	4	4	3	3	2	3
7211 Call centre agents/operators	3	1.1	4	4	3	3	2	3
7212 Customer care occupations	3	1.1	4	4	3	3	2	3
8111 Food, drink and tobacco process operatives	6	1.1	4	4	6	6	5	6
8112 Glass and ceramics process operatives	6	1.1	4	4	6	6	5	6
8113 Textile process operatives	7	1.1	4	4	7	7	5	7
8114 Chemical and related process operatives	5	1.1	4	4	5	5	5	5
8115 Rubber process operatives	6	1.1	4	4	6	6	5	6
8116 Plastics process operatives	6	1.1	4	4	6	6	5	6
8117 Metal making and treating process operatives	6	1.1	4	4	6	6	5	6
8118 Electroplaters	6	1.1	4	4	6	6	5	6

Please note: This derivation table has no empty cells. The shaded cells have been filled using the priority order rules. See Appendix A.

Table 11 - *continued*

Standard Occupational Classification 2000 unit group		Simplified NS-SEC	Employment status/size of organisation						
			1 Employers - large organisations	2 Employers - small organisations	3 Self-employed, no employees	4 Managers - large organisations	5 Managers - small organisations	6 Supervisors	7 Other employees
8119	Process operatives n.e.c.	6	1.1	4	4	6	6	5	6
8121	Paper and wood machine operatives	6	1.1	4	4	6	6	5	6
8122	Coal mine operatives	7	1.1	4	4	7	7	5	7
8123	Quarry workers and related operatives	5	1.1	4	4	5	5	5	5
8124	Energy plant operatives	6	1.1	4	4	6	6	5	6
8125	Metal working machine operatives	6	1.1	4	4	6	6	5	6
8126	Water and sewerage plant operatives	5	1.1	4	4	5	5	5	5
8129	Plant and machine operatives n.e.c.	6	1.1	4	4	6	6	5	6
8131	Assemblers (electrical products)	6	1.1	4	4	6	6	5	6
8132	Assemblers (vehicles and metal goods)	6	1.1	4	4	6	6	5	6
8133	Routine inspectors and testers	5	1.1	4	4	5	5	5	5
8134	Weighers, graders, sorters	7	1.1	4	4	7	7	5	7
8135	Tyre, exhaust and windscreen fitters	6	1.1	4	4	6	6	5	6
8136	Clothing cutters	6	1.1	4	4	6	6	5	6
8137	Sewing machinists	7	1.1	4	4	7	7	5	7
8138	Routine laboratory testers	3	1.1	4	4	3	3	2	3
8139	Assemblers and routine operatives n.e.c.	7	1.1	4	4	7	7	5	7
8141	Scaffolders, stagers, riggers	6	1.1	4	4	6	6	5	6
8142	Road construction operatives	5	1.1	4	4	6	6	5	6
8143	Rail construction and maintenance operatives	5	1.1	4	4	5	5	5	5
8149	Construction operatives n.e.c.	5	1.1	4	4	7	7	5	7
8211	Heavy goods vehicle drivers	7	1.1	4	4	7	7	5	7
8212	Van drivers	7	1.1	4	4	7	7	5	7
8213	Bus and coach drivers	7	1.1	4	4	7	7	5	7
8214	Taxi, cab drivers and chauffeurs	4	1.1	4	4	7	7	5	7
8215	Driving instructors	4	1.1	4	4	6	6	5	6
8216	Rail transport operatives	5	1.1	4	4	5	5	5	5
8217	Seafarers (merchant navy); barge, lighter and boat operatives	6	1.1	4	4	6	6	5	6
8218	Air transport operatives	5	1.1	4	4	5	5	5	5
8219	Transport operatives n.e.c.	5	1.1	4	4	5	5	5	5
8221	Crane drivers	6	1.1	4	4	6	6	5	6
8222	Fork-lift truck drivers	6	1.1	4	4	6	6	5	6
8223	Agricultural machinery drivers	6	1.1	4	4	6	6	5	6
8229	Mobile machine drivers and operatives n.e.c.	7	1.1	4	4	7	7	5	7
9111	Farm workers	6	1.1	4	4	6	6	5	6
9112	Forestry workers	4	1.1	4	4	6	6	5	6
9119	Fishing and agriculture related occupations n.e.c.	7	1.1	4	4	7	7	5	7
9121	Labourers in building and woodworking trades	7	1.1	4	4	7	7	5	7
9129	Labourers in other construction trades n.e.c.	7	1.1	4	4	7	7	5	7
9131	Labourers in foundries	7	1.1	4	4	7	7	5	7
9132	Industrial cleaning process occupations	7	1.1	4	4	7	7	5	7
9133	Printing machine minders and assistants	6	1.1	4	4	6	6	5	6
9134	Packers, bottlers, canners, fillers	7	1.1	4	4	7	7	5	7
9139	Labourers in process and plant operations n.e.c.	7	1.1	4	4	7	7	5	7
9141	Stevedores, dockers and slingers	7	1.1	4	4	7	7	5	7
9149	Other goods handling and storage occupations n.e.c.	7	1.1	4	4	7	7	5	7
9211	Postal workers, mail sorters, messengers, couriers	6	1.1	4	4	6	6	5	6
9219	Elementary office occupations n.e.c.	6	1.1	4	4	6	6	5	6
9221	Hospital porters	6	1.1	4	4	6	6	5	6
9222	Hotel porters	7	1.1	4	4	7	7	5	7
9223	Kitchen and catering assistants	6	1.1	4	4	6	6	5	6
9224	Waiters, waitresses	7	1.1	4	4	7	7	5	7
9225	Bar staff	7	1.1	4	4	7	7	5	7
9226	Leisure and theme park attendants	7	1.1	4	4	7	7	5	7
9229	Elementary personal services occupations n.e.c.	7	1.1	4	4	7	7	5	7
9231	Window cleaners	4	1.1	4	4	7	7	5	7
9232	Road sweepers	7	1.1	4	4	7	7	5	7
9233	Cleaners, domestics	7	1.1	4	4	7	7	5	7
9234	Launderers, dry cleaners, pressers	7	1.1	4	4	7	7	5	7
9235	Refuse and salvage occupations	7	1.1	4	4	7	7	5	7

Please note: This derivation table has no empty cells. The shaded cells have been filled using the priority order rules. See Appendix A.

Table 11 - *continued*

Standard Occupational Classification 2000 unit group	Simplified NS-SEC	Employment status/size of organisation						
		1 Employers - large organisations	2 Employers - small organisations	3 Self-employed, no employees	4 Managers - large organisations	5 Managers - small organisations	6 Supervisors	7 Other employees
9239 Elementary cleaning occupations n.e.c.	7	1.1	4	4	7	7	5	7
9241 Security guards and related occupations	6	1.1	4	4	6	6	5	6
9242 Traffic wardens	6	5	5	6	6	6	5	6
9243 School crossing patrol attendants	7	5	5	7	7	7	5	7
9244 School mid-day assistants	7	5	5	7	7	7	5	7
9245 Car park attendants	7	1.1	4	4	7	7	5	7
9249 Elementary security occupations n.e.c.	6	1.1	4	4	6	6	5	6
9251 Shelf fillers	6	1.1	4	4	6	6	5	6
9259 Elementary sales occupations n.e.c.	6	1.1	4	4	6	6	5	6

Please note: This derivation table has no empty cells. The shaded cells have been filled using the priority order rules. See Appendix A.

Table **12**

NS-SEC based on SOC2000 simplified and reduced derivation table: operational categories

Standard Occupational Classification 2000 unit group		Simplified NS-SEC	Employment status				
			1 Employers	2 Self-employed - no employees	3 Managers	4 Supervisors	5 Other employees
1111	Senior officials in national government	2	2	2	2	2	2
1112	Directors and chief executives of major organisations	2	1	1	2	2	2
1113	Senior officials in local government	2	9.1	9.1	2	2	2
1114	Senior officials of special interest organisations	5	8.1	9.1	5	5	5
1121	Production, works and maintenance managers	2	8.1	9.1	2	2	2
1122	Managers in construction	5	8.1	9.1	5	5	5
1123	Managers in mining and energy	2	8.1	9.1	2	2	2
1131	Financial managers and chartered secretaries	2	3.3	3.3	2	2	2
1132	Marketing and sales managers	2	8.1	9.1	2	2	2
1133	Purchasing managers	2	8.1	9.1	2	2	2
1134	Advertising and public relations managers	2	8.1	9.1	2	2	2
1135	Personnel, training and industrial relations managers	2	8.1	9.1	2	2	2
1136	Information and communication technology managers	2	8.1	9.1	2	2	2
1137	Research and development managers	2	3.3	3.3	2	2	2
1141	Quality assurance managers	5	8.1	9.1	5	5	5
1142	Customer care managers	5	8.1	9.1	5	5	5
1151	Financial institution managers	5	8.1	9.1	5	5	5
1152	Office managers	5	8.1	9.1	5	5	5
1161	Transport and distribution managers	5	8.1	9.1	5	5	5
1162	Storage and warehouse managers	5	8.1	9.1	5	5	5
1163	Retail and wholesale managers	5	8.1	9.1	5	5	5
1171	Officers in armed forces	2	2	2	2	2	2
1172	Police officers (inspectors and above)	2	2	2	2	2	2
1173	Senior officers in fire, ambulance, prison and related services	2	2	2	2	2	2
1174	Security managers	5	8.1	9.1	5	5	5
1181	Hospital and health service managers	2	8.1	9.1	2	2	2
1182	Pharmacy managers	5	3.3	3.3	5	5	5
1183	Healthcare practice managers	5	8.1	9.1	5	5	5
1184	Social services managers	2	8.1	9.1	2	2	2
1185	Residential and day care managers	5	8.1	9.1	5	5	5
1211	Farm managers	5	8.2	9.2	5	5	5
1212	Natural environment and conservation managers	2	8.1	9.1	2	2	2
1219	Managers in animal husbandry, forestry and fishing n.e.c.	9.2	8.2	9.2	5	5	5
1221	Hotel and accommodation managers	9.1	8.1	9.1	5	5	5
1222	Conference and exhibition managers	5	8.1	9.1	5	5	5
1223	Restaurant and catering managers	8.1	8.1	9.1	5	5	5
1224	Publicans and managers of licensed premises	5	8.1	9.1	5	5	5
1225	Leisure and sports managers	5	8.1	9.1	5	5	5
1226	Travel agency managers	5	8.1	9.1	5	5	5
1231	Property, housing and land managers	2	8.1	9.1	2	2	2
1232	Garage managers and proprietors	8.1	8.1	9.1	5	5	5
1233	Hairdressing and beauty salon managers and proprietors	8.1	8.1	9.1	5	5	5
1234	Shopkeepers and wholesale retail dealers	8.1	8.1	9.1	5	5	5
1235	Recycling and refuse disposal managers	5	8.1	9.1	5	5	5
1239	Managers and proprietors in other services n.e.c.	5	8.1	9.1	5	5	5
2111	Chemists	3.1	3.3	3.3	3.1	3.1	3.1
2112	Biological scientists and biochemists	3.1	3.3	3.3	3.1	3.1	3.1
2113	Physicists, geologists and meteorologists	3.1	3.3	3.3	3.1	3.1	3.1
2121	Civil engineers	3.1	3.3	3.3	3.1	3.1	3.1
2122	Mechanical engineers	3.1	3.3	3.3	3.1	3.1	3.1
2123	Electrical engineers	3.1	3.3	3.3	3.1	3.1	3.1
2124	Electronics engineers	3.1	3.3	3.3	3.1	3.1	3.1
2125	Chemical engineers	3.1	3.3	3.3	3.1	3.1	3.1
2126	Design and development engineers	3.1	3.3	3.3	3.1	3.1	3.1
2127	Production and process engineers	4.1	4.3	4.3	4.1	4.1	4.1
2128	Planning and quality control engineers	4.1	4.3	4.3	4.1	4.1	4.1
2129	Engineering professionals n.e.c.	3.1	3.3	3.3	3.1	3.1	3.1
2131	IT strategy and planning professionals	3.2	3.4	3.4	3.2	3.2	3.2

Please note: This derivation table has no empty cells. The shaded cells have been filled using the priority order rules. See Appendix A.

Table 12 - *continued*

Standard Occupational Classification 2000 unit group		Simplified NS-SEC	Employment status				
			1 Employers	2 Self-employed - no employees	3 Managers	4 Supervisors	5 Other employees
2132	Software professionals	3.2	3.4	3.4	3.2	3.2	3.2
2211	Medical practitioners	3.1	3.3	3.3	3.1	3.1	3.1
2212	Psychologists	3.1	3.3	3.3	3.1	3.1	3.1
2213	Pharmacists/pharmacologists	3.1	3.3	3.3	3.1	3.1	3.1
2214	Ophthalmic opticians	4.1	4.3	4.3	4.1	4.1	4.1
2215	Dental practitioners	3.3	3.3	3.3	3.1	3.1	3.1
2216	Veterinarians	3.1	3.3	3.3	3.1	3.1	3.1
2311	Higher education teaching professionals	3.1	3.3	3.3	3.1	3.1	3.1
2312	Further education teaching professionals	4.1	4.3	4.3	4.1	4.1	4.1
2313	Education officers, school inspectors	3.1	3.1	3.1	3.1	3.1	3.1
2314	Secondary education teaching professionals	4.1	4.3	4.3	4.1	4.1	4.1
2315	Primary and nursery education teaching professionals	4.1	4.3	4.3	4.1	4.1	4.1
2316	Special needs education teaching professionals	4.1	4.3	4.3	4.1	4.1	4.1
2317	Registrars and senior administrators of educational establishments	3.1	3.1	3.1	3.1	3.1	3.1
2319	Teaching professionals n.e.c.	9.1	8.1	9.1	7.3	6	7.3
2321	Scientific researchers	3.1	3.3	3.3	3.1	3.1	3.1
2322	Social science researchers	3.1	3.3	3.3	3.1	3.1	3.1
2329	Researchers n.e.c.	3.1	3.3	3.3	3.1	3.1	3.1
2411	Solicitors and lawyers, judges and coroners	3.1	3.3	3.3	3.1	3.1	3.1
2419	Legal professionals n.e.c.	3.1	3.3	3.3	3.1	3.1	3.1
2421	Chartered and certified accountants	3.1	3.3	3.3	3.1	3.1	3.1
2422	Management accountants	3.2	3.4	3.4	3.2	3.2	3.2
2423	Management consultants, actuaries, economists and statisticians	3.1	3.3	3.3	3.1	3.1	3.1
2431	Architects	3.1	3.3	3.3	3.1	3.1	3.1
2432	Town planners	3.1	3.3	3.3	3.1	3.1	3.1
2433	Quantity surveyors	4.1	4.3	4.3	4.1	4.1	4.1
2434	Chartered surveyors (not quantity surveyors)	3.1	3.3	3.3	3.1	3.1	3.1
2441	Public service administrative professionals	4.1	4.1	4.1	4.1	4.1	4.1
2442	Social workers	4.1	4.3	4.3	4.1	4.1	4.1
2443	Probation officers	3.2	3.2	3.2	3.2	3.2	3.2
2444	Clergy	3.1	3.3	3.3	3.1	3.1	3.1
2451	Librarians	4.1	4.3	4.3	4.1	4.1	4.1
2452	Archivists and curators	4.1	4.3	4.3	4.1	4.1	4.1
3111	Laboratory technicians	4.1	4.3	4.3	4.1	4.1	4.1
3112	Electrical/electronics technicians	7.3	8.1	9.1	7.3	6	7.3
3113	Engineering technicians	4.1	4.3	4.3	4.1	4.1	4.1
3114	Building and civil engineering technicians	4.1	4.3	4.3	4.1	4.1	4.1
3115	Quality assurance technicians	11.1	8.1	9.1	11.1	10	11.1
3119	Science and engineering technicians n.e.c.	4.1	4.3	4.3	4.1	4.1	4.1
3121	Architectural technologists and town planning technicians	4.1	4.3	4.3	4.1	4.1	4.1
3122	Draughtspersons	7.3	8.1	9.1	7.3	6	7.3
3123	Building inspectors	4.1	4.3	4.3	4.1	4.1	4.1
3131	IT operations technicians	4.1	4.3	4.3	4.1	4.1	4.1
3132	IT user support technicians	4.1	4.3	4.3	4.1	4.1	4.1
3211	Nurses	4.1	4.3	4.3	4.1	4.1	4.1
3212	Midwives	4.1	4.3	4.3	4.1	4.1	4.1
3213	Paramedics	6	6	7.2	7.2	6	7.2
3214	Medical radiographers	4.1	4.3	4.3	4.1	4.1	4.1
3215	Chiropodists	4.1	4.3	4.3	4.1	4.1	4.1
3216	Dispensing opticians	7.3	8.1	9.1	7.3	6	7.3
3217	Pharmaceutical dispensers	12.1	8.1	9.1	12.1	10	12.1
3218	Medical and dental technicians	7.3	8.1	9.1	7.3	6	7.3
3221	Physiotherapists	4.1	4.3	4.3	4.1	4.1	4.1
3222	Occupational therapists	4.1	4.3	4.3	4.1	4.1	4.1
3223	Speech and language therapists	3.2	3.4	3.4	3.2	3.2	3.2
3229	Therapists n.e.c.	4.3	4.3	4.3	4.1	4.1	4.1
3231	Youth and community workers	4.1	4.3	4.3	4.1	4.1	4.1
3232	Housing and welfare officers	4.1	4.3	4.3	4.1	4.1	4.1
3311	NCOs and other ranks	7.2	6	7.2	7.2	6	7.2
3312	Police officers (sergeant and below)	7.2	6	7.2	7.2	6	7.2
3313	Fire service officers (leading fire officer and below)	7.2	6	7.2	7.2	6	7.2
3314	Prison service officers (below principal officer)	7.2	6	7.2	7.2	6	7.2
3319	Protective service associate professionals n.e.c.	4.1	4.1	4.1	4.1	4.1	4.1
3411	Artists	4.3	4.3	4.3	4.1	4.1	4.1
3412	Authors, writers	4.3	4.3	4.3	4.1	4.1	4.1
3413	Actors, entertainers	4.3	4.3	4.3	4.1	4.1	4.1
3414	Dancers and choreographers	4.3	4.3	4.3	4.1	4.1	4.1
3415	Musicians	4.3	4.3	4.3	4.1	4.1	4.1

Please note: This derivation table has no empty cells. The shaded cells have been filled using the priority order rules. See Appendix A.

Table 12 - *continued*

Standard Occupational Classification 2000 unit group		Simplified NS-SEC	Employment status				
			1 Employers	2 Self-employed - no employees	3 Managers	4 Supervisors	5 Other employees
3416	Arts officers, producers and directors	4.3	4.3	4.3	4.1	4.1	4.1
3421	Graphic designers	7.3	8.1	9.1	7.3	6	7.3
3422	Product, clothing and related designers	9.1	8.1	9.1	7.3	6	7.3
3431	Journalists, newspaper and periodical editors	4.1	4.3	4.3	4.1	4.1	4.1
3432	Broadcasting associate professionals	4.1	4.3	4.3	4.1	4.1	4.1
3433	Public relations officers	4.1	4.3	4.3	4.1	4.1	4.1
3434	Photographers and audio-visual equipment operators	7.2	8.1	9.1	7.2	6	7.2
3441	Sports players	4.1	4.3	4.3	4.1	4.1	4.1
3442	Sports coaches, instructors and officials	4.1	4.3	4.3	4.1	4.1	4.1
3443	Fitness instructors	12.2	8.1	9.1	12.2	10	12.2
3449	Sports and fitness occupations n.e.c.	7.2	8.1	9.1	7.2	6	7.2
3511	Air traffic controllers	4.1	4.1	4.1	4.1	4.1	4.1
3512	Aircraft pilots and flight engineers	3.2	3.4	3.4	3.2	3.2	3.2
3513	Ship and hovercraft officers	4.1	4.3	4.3	4.1	4.1	4.1
3514	Train drivers	11.1	10	11.1	11.1	10	11.1
3520	Legal associate professionals	7.1	8.1	9.1	7.1	6	7.1
3531	Estimators, valuers and assessors	4.1	4.3	4.3	4.1	4.1	4.1
3532	Brokers	3.2	3.4	3.4	3.2	3.2	3.2
3533	Insurance underwriters	3.2	3.4	3.4	3.2	3.2	3.2
3534	Finance and investment analysts/advisers	4.1	4.3	4.3	4.1	4.1	4.1
3535	Taxation experts	3.2	3.4	3.4	3.2	3.2	3.2
3536	Importers, exporters	4.2	4.4	4.4	4.2	4.2	4.2
3537	Financial and accounting technicians	4.2	4.4	4.4	4.2	4.2	4.2
3539	Business and related associate professionals n.e.c.	4.1	4.3	4.3	4.1	4.1	4.1
3541	Buyers and purchasing officers	4.1	4.3	4.3	4.1	4.1	4.1
3542	Sales representatives	4.2	4.4	4.4	4.2	4.2	4.2
3543	Marketing associate professionals	4.1	4.3	4.3	4.1	4.1	4.1
3544	Estate agents, auctioneers	4.1	4.3	4.3	4.1	4.1	4.1
3551	Conservation and environmental protection officers	3.1	3.3	3.3	3.1	3.1	3.1
3552	Countryside and park rangers	7.2	8.1	9.1	7.2	6	7.2
3561	Public service associate professionals	4.1	4.1	4.1	4.1	4.1	4.1
3562	Personnel and industrial relations officers	4.1	4.3	4.3	4.1	4.1	4.1
3563	Vocational and industrial trainers and instructors	4.1	4.3	4.3	4.1	4.1	4.1
3564	Careers advisers and vocational guidance specialists	4.1	4.3	4.3	4.1	4.1	4.1
3565	Inspectors of factories, utilities and trading standards	4.1	4.1	4.1	4.1	4.1	4.1
3566	Statutory examiners	4.1	4.1	4.1	4.1	4.1	4.1
3567	Occupational hygienists and safety officers (health and safety)	4.1	4.3	4.3	4.1	4.1	4.1
3568	Environmental health officers	3.2	3.2	3.2	3.2	3.2	3.2
4111	Civil Service executive officers	4.1	4.1	4.1	4.1	4.1	4.1
4112	Civil Service administrative officers and assistants	7.1	6	7.1	7.1	6	7.1
4113	Local government clerical officers and assistants	7.1	6	7.1	7.1	6	7.1
4114	Officers of non-governmental organisations	4.1	4.3	4.3	4.1	4.1	4.1
4121	Credit controllers	7.1	8.1	9.1	7.1	6	7.1
4122	Accounts and wages clerks, book-keepers, other financial clerks	7.1	8.1	9.1	7.1	6	7.1
4123	Counter clerks	7.1	8.1	9.1	7.1	6	7.1
4131	Filing and other records assistants/clerks	7.1	8.1	9.1	7.1	6	7.1
4132	Pensions and insurance clerks	7.1	8.1	9.1	7.1	6	7.1
4133	Stock control clerks	12.6	8.1	9.1	12.6	10	12.6
4134	Transport and distribution clerks	7.1	8.1	9.1	7.1	6	7.1
4135	Library assistants/clerks	7.1	8.1	9.1	7.1	6	7.1
4136	Database assistants/clerks	7.1	8.1	9.1	7.1	6	7.1
4137	Market research interviewers	12.6	8.1	9.1	12.6	10	12.6
4141	Telephonists	12.6	8.1	9.1	12.6	10	12.6
4142	Communication operators	11.1	8.1	9.1	11.1	10	11.1
4150	General office assistants/clerks	7.2	8.1	9.1	7.2	6	7.2
4211	Medical secretaries	7.1	8.1	9.1	7.1	6	7.1
4212	Legal secretaries	7.1	8.1	9.1	7.1	6	7.1
4213	School secretaries	7.1	8.1	9.1	7.1	6	7.1
4214	Company secretaries	7.1	8.1	9.1	7.1	6	7.1
4215	Personal assistants and other secretaries	7.1	8.1	9.1	7.1	6	7.1
4216	Receptionists	12.6	8.1	9.1	12.6	10	12.6
4217	Typists	7.1	8.1	9.1	7.1	6	7.1
5111	Farmers	9.2	8.2	9.2	6	6	6
5112	Horticultural trades	12.5	8.2	9.2	12.5	10	12.5

Please note: This derivation table has no empty cells. The shaded cells have been filled using the priority order rules. See Appendix A.

Table 12 - *continued*

Standard Occupational Classification 2000 unit group		Simplified NS-SEC	Employment status				
			1 Employers	2 Self-employed - no employees	3 Managers	4 Supervisors	5 Other employees
5113	Gardeners and groundsmen/groundswomen	11.1	8.1	9.1	11.1	10	11.1
5119	Agricultural and fishing trades n.e.c.	9.2	8.2	9.2	11.1	10	11.1
5211	Smiths and forge workers	13.3	8.1	9.1	13.3	10	13.3
5212	Moulders, core makers, die casters	12.3	8.1	9.1	12.3	10	12.3
5213	Sheet metal workers	12.3	8.1	9.1	12.3	10	12.3
5214	Metal plate workers, shipwrights, riveters	13.3	8.1	9.1	13.3	10	13.3
5215	Welding trades	13.3	8.1	9.1	13.3	10	13.3
5216	Pipe fitters	13.3	8.1	9.1	13.3	10	13.3
5221	Metal machining setters and setter-operators	12.3	8.1	9.1	12.3	10	12.3
5222	Tool makers, tool fitters and markers-out	11.1	8.1	9.1	11.1	10	11.1
5223	Metal working production and maintenance fitters	11.1	8.1	9.1	11.1	10	11.1
5224	Precision instrument makers and repairers	11.1	8.1	9.1	11.1	10	11.1
5231	Motor mechanics, auto engineers	11.1	8.1	9.1	11.1	10	11.1
5232	Vehicle body builders and repairers	11.1	8.1	9.1	11.1	10	11.1
5233	Auto electricians	11.1	8.1	9.1	11.1	10	11.1
5234	Vehicle spray painters	12.3	8.1	9.1	12.3	10	12.3
5241	Electricians, electrical fitters	11.1	8.1	9.1	11.1	10	11.1
5242	Telecommunications engineers	7.4	8.1	9.1	7.4	6	7.4
5243	Lines repairers and cable jointers	11.1	8.1	9.1	11.1	10	11.1
5244	TV, video and audio engineers	11.1	8.1	9.1	11.1	10	11.1
5245	Computer engineers, installation and maintenance	7.4	8.1	9.1	7.4	6	7.4
5249	Electrical/electronics engineers n.e.c.	7.4	8.1	9.1	7.4	6	7.4
5311	Steel erectors	12.3	8.1	9.1	12.3	10	12.3
5312	Bricklayers, masons	9.1	8.1	9.1	13.3	10	13.3
5313	Roofers, roof tilers and slaters	9.1	8.1	9.1	13.2	10	13.2
5314	Plumbers, heating and ventilating engineers	11.1	8.1	9.1	11.1	10	11.1
5315	Carpenters and joiners	9.1	8.1	9.1	13.3	10	13.3
5316	Glaziers, window fabricators and fitters	9.1	8.1	9.1	13.2	10	13.2
5319	Construction trades n.e.c.	9.1	8.1	9.1	12.4	10	12.4
5321	Plasterers	9.1	8.1	9.1	13.3	10	13.3
5322	Floorers and wall tilers	9.1	8.1	9.1	13.3	10	13.3
5323	Painters and decorators	9.1	8.1	9.1	13.3	10	13.3
5411	Weavers and knitters	13.3	8.1	9.1	13.3	10	13.3
5412	Upholsterers	13.3	8.1	9.1	12.3	10	12.3
5413	Leather and related trades	13.3	8.1	9.1	12.3	10	13.3
5414	Tailors and dressmakers	12.3	8.1	9.1	12.3	10	12.3
5419	Textiles, garments and related trades n.e.c.	13.3	8.1	9.1	13.3	10	13.3
5421	Originators, compositors and print preparers	11.1	8.1	9.1	11.1	10	11.1
5422	Printers	11.1	8.1	9.1	11.1	10	11.1
5423	Bookbinders and print finishers	13.3	8.1	9.1	13.3	10	13.3
5424	Screen printers	11.1	8.1	9.1	11.1	10	11.1
5431	Butchers, meat cutters	13.3	8.1	9.1	13.3	10	13.3
5432	Bakers, flour confectioners	11.1	8.1	9.1	11.1	10	11.1
5433	Fishmongers, poultry dressers	13.3	8.1	9.1	13.3	10	13.3
5434	Chefs, cooks	12.2	8.1	9.1	12.2	10	12.2
5491	Glass and ceramics makers, decorators and finishers	13.3	8.1	9.1	13.3	10	13.3
5492	Furniture makers, other craft woodworkers	13.3	8.1	9.1	13.3	10	13.3
5493	Pattern makers (moulds)	11.1	8.1	9.1	11.1	10	11.1
5494	Musical instrument makers and tuners	9.1	8.1	9.1	11.1	10	11.1
5495	Goldsmiths, silversmiths, precious stone workers	11.1	8.1	9.1	11.1	10	11.1
5496	Floral arrangers, florists	13.1	8.1	9.1	13.1	10	13.1
5499	Hand craft occupations n.e.c.	11.1	8.1	9.1	11.1	10	11.1
6111	Nursing auxiliaries and assistants	7.3	8.1	9.1	7.3	6	7.3
6112	Ambulance staff (excluding paramedics)	7.2	6	7.2	7.2	6	7.2
6113	Dental nurses	12.2	8.1	9.1	12.2	10	12.2
6114	Houseparents and residential wardens	12.7	8.1	9.1	12.7	10	12.7
6115	Care assistants and home carers	12.2	8.1	9.1	12.2	10	12.2
6121	Nursery nurses	7.2	8.1	9.1	7.2	6	7.2
6122	Childminders and related occupations	9.1	8.1	9.1	13.1	10	13.1
6123	Playgroup leaders/assistants	12.7	8.1	9.1	12.7	10	12.7
6124	Educational assistants	12.7	8.1	9.1	12.7	10	12.7
6131	Veterinary nurses and assistants	12.2	8.1	9.1	12.2	10	12.2
6139	Animal care occupations n.e.c.	13.5	8.2	9.2	13.5	10	13.5
6211	Sports and leisure assistants	12.2	8.1	9.1	12.2	10	12.2
6212	Travel agents	7.2	8.1	9.1	7.2	6	7.2
6213	Travel and tour guides	13.1	8.1	9.1	13.1	10	13.1
6214	Air travel assistants	7.2	8.1	9.1	7.2	6	7.2
6215	Rail travel assistants	7.2	8.1	9.1	7.2	6	7.2
6219	Leisure and travel service occupations n.e.c.	13.3	8.1	9.1	13.3	10	13.3
6221	Hairdressers, barbers	13.1	8.1	9.1	13.1	10	13.1

Please note: This derivation table has no empty cells. The shaded cells have been filled using the priority order rules. See Appendix A.

Table 12 - *continued*

Standard Occupational Classification 2000 unit group		Simplified NS-SEC	Employment status				
			1 Employers	2 Self-employed - no employees	3 Managers	4 Supervisors	5 Other employees
6222	Beauticians and related occupations	9.1	8.1	9.1	12.2	10	12.2
6231	Housekeepers and related occupations	12.2	8.1	9.1	12.2	10	12.2
6232	Caretakers	12.2	8.1	9.1	12.2	10	12.2
6291	Undertakers and mortuary assistants	12.2	8.1	9.1	12.2	10	12.2
6292	Pest control officers	12.2	8.1	9.1	12.2	10	12.2
7111	Sales and retail assistants	12.1	8.1	9.1	12.1	10	12.1
7112	Retail cashiers and check-out operators	12.1	8.1	9.1	12.1	10	12.1
7113	Telephone salespersons	12.1	8.1	9.1	12.1	10	12.1
7121	Collector salespersons and credit agents	12.1	8.1	9.1	12.1	10	12.1
7122	Debt, rent and other cash collectors	7.2	8.1	9.1	7.2	6	7.2
7123	Roundsmen/women and van salespersons	13.3	8.1	9.1	13.3	10	13.3
7124	Market and street traders and assistants	9.1	8.1	9.1	13.1	10	13.1
7125	Merchandisers and window dressers	7.2	8.1	9.1	7.2	6	7.2
7129	Sales related occupations n.e.c.	7.2	8.1	9.1	7.2	6	7.2
7211	Call centre agents/operators	7.2	8.1	9.1	7.2	6	7.2
7212	Customer care occupations	7.2	8.1	9.1	7.2	6	7.2
8111	Food, drink and tobacco process operatives	12.4	8.1	9.1	12.4	10	12.4
8112	Glass and ceramics process operatives	12.3	8.1	9.1	12.3	10	12.3
8113	Textile process operatives	13.2	8.1	9.1	13.2	10	13.2
8114	Chemical and related process operatives	11.2	8.1	9.1	11.2	10	11.2
8115	Rubber process operatives	12.3	8.1	9.1	12.3	10	12.3
8116	Plastics process operatives	12.4	8.1	9.1	12.4	10	12.4
8117	Metal making and treating process operatives	12.3	8.1	9.1	12.3	10	12.3
8118	Electroplaters	12.3	8.1	9.1	12.3	10	12.3
8119	Process operatives n.e.c.	12.4	8.1	9.1	12.4	10	12.4
8121	Paper and wood machine operatives	12.3	8.1	9.1	12.3	10	12.3
8122	Coal mine operatives	13.3	8.1	9.1	13.3	10	13.3
8123	Quarry workers and related operatives	11.2	8.1	9.1	11.2	10	11.2
8124	Energy plant operatives	12.4	8.1	9.1	12.4	10	12.4
8125	Metal working machine operatives	12.4	8.1	9.1	12.4	10	12.4
8126	Water and sewerage plant operatives	11.2	8.1	9.1	11.2	10	11.2
8129	Plant and machine operatives n.e.c.	12.4	8.1	9.1	12.4	10	12.4
8131	Assemblers (electrical products)	12.4	8.1	9.1	12.4	10	12.4
8132	Assemblers (vehicles and metal goods)	12.4	8.1	9.1	12.4	10	12.4
8133	Routine inspectors and testers	11.2	8.1	9.1	11.2	10	11.2
8134	Weighers, graders, sorters	13.2	8.1	9.1	13.2	10	13.2
8135	Tyre, exhaust and windscreen fitters	12.4	8.1	9.1	12.4	10	12.4
8136	Clothing cutters	12.3	8.1	9.1	12.3	10	12.3
8137	Sewing machinists	13.2	8.1	9.1	13.2	10	13.2
8138	Routine laboratory testers	7.3	8.1	9.1	7.3	6	7.3
8139	Assemblers and routine operatives n.e.c.	13.2	8.1	9.1	13.2	10	13.2
8141	Scaffolders, stagers, riggers	12.4	8.1	9.1	12.4	10	12.4
8142	Road construction operatives	10	8.1	9.1	12.4	10	12.4
8143	Rail construction and maintenance operatives	11.2	8.1	9.1	11.2	10	11.2
8149	Construction operatives n.e.c.	10	8.1	9.1	13.4	10	13.4
8211	Heavy goods vehicle drivers	13.3	8.1	9.1	13.3	10	13.3
8212	Van drivers	13.3	8.1	9.1	13.3	10	13.3
8213	Bus and coach drivers	13.3	8.1	9.1	13.3	10	13.3
8214	Taxi, cab drivers and chauffeurs	9.1	8.1	9.1	13.3	10	13.3
8215	Driving instructors	9.1	8.1	9.1	12.2	10	12.2
8216	Rail transport operatives	11.2	8.1	9.1	11.2	10	11.2
8217	Seafarers (merchant navy); barge, lighter and boat operatives	12.4	8.1	9.1	12.4	10	12.4
8218	Air transport operatives	11.2	8.1	9.1	11.2	10	11.2
8219	Transport operatives n.e.c.	10	8.1	9.1	11.2	10	11.2
8221	Crane drivers	12.3	8.1	9.1	12.3	10	12.3
8222	Fork-lift truck drivers	12.3	8.1	9.1	12.3	10	12.3
8223	Agricultural machinery drivers	12.5	8.2	9.2	12.5	10	12.5
8229	Mobile machine drivers and operatives n.e.c.	13.3	8.1	9.1	13.3	10	13.3
9111	Farm workers	12.5	8.2	9.2	12.5	10	12.5
9112	Forestry workers	9.2	8.2	9.2	12.5	10	12.5
9119	Fishing and agriculture related occupations n.e.c.	13.5	8.2	9.2	13.5	10	13.5
9121	Labourers in building and woodworking trades	13.4	8.1	9.1	13.4	10	13.4
9129	Labourers in other construction trades n.e.c.	13.4	8.1	9.1	13.4	10	13.4
9131	Labourers in foundries	13.4	8.1	9.1	13.4	10	13.4
9132	Industrial cleaning process occupations	13.4	8.1	9.1	13.4	10	13.4
9133	Printing machine minders and assistants	12.3	8.1	9.1	12.3	10	12.3
9134	Packers, bottlers, canners, fillers	13.2	8.1	9.1	13.2	10	13.2
9139	Labourers in process and plant operations n.e.c.	13.4	8.1	9.1	13.4	10	13.4
9141	Stevedores, dockers and slingers	13.4	8.1	9.1	13.4	10	13.4
9149	Other goods handling and storage occupations n.e.c.	13.4	8.1	9.1	13.4	10	13.4

Please note: This derivation table has no empty cells. The shaded cells have been filled using the priority order rules. See Appendix A.

Table 12 - *continued*

Standard Occupational Classification 2000 unit group		Simplified NS-SEC	Employment status				
			1 Employers	2 Self-employed - no employees	3 Managers	4 Supervisors	5 Other employees
9211	Postal workers, mail sorters, messengers, couriers	12.2	8.1	9.1	12.2	10	12.2
9219	Elementary office occupations n.e.c.	12.6	8.1	9.1	12.6	10	12.6
9221	Hospital porters	12.2	8.1	9.1	12.2	10	12.2
9222	Hotel porters	13.1	8.1	9.1	13.1	10	13.1
9223	Kitchen and catering assistants	12.2	8.1	9.1	12.2	10	12.2
9224	Waiters, waitresses	13.1	8.1	9.1	13.1	10	13.1
9225	Bar staff	13.1	8.1	9.1	13.1	10	13.1
9226	Leisure and theme park attendants	13.1	8.1	9.1	13.1	10	13.1
9229	Elementary personal services occupations n.e.c.	13.1	8.1	9.1	13.1	10	13.1
9231	Window cleaners	9.1	8.1	9.1	13.2	10	13.2
9232	Road sweepers	13.4	8.1	9.1	13.4	10	13.4
9233	Cleaners, domestics	13.4	8.1	9.1	13.4	10	13.4
9234	Launderers, dry cleaners, pressers	13.2	8.1	9.1	13.2	10	13.2
9235	Refuse and salvage occupations	13.4	8.1	9.1	13.4	10	13.4
9239	Elementary cleaning occupations n.e.c.	13.4	8.1	9.1	13.4	10	13.4
9241	Security guards and related occupations	12.2	8.1	9.1	12.2	10	12.2
9242	Traffic wardens	12.2	10	12.2	12.2	10	12.2
9243	School crossing patrol attendants	13.1	10	13.1	13.1	10	13.1
9244	School mid-day assistants	13.1	10	13.1	13.1	10	13.1
9245	Car park attendants	13.4	8.1	9.1	13.4	10	13.4
9249	Elementary security occupations n.e.c.	12.2	8.1	9.1	12.2	10	12.2
9251	Shelf fillers	12.1	8.1	9.1	12.1	10	12.1
9259	Elementary sales occupations n.e.c.	12.1	8.1	9.1	12.1	10	12.1

Please note: This derivation table has no empty cells. The shaded cells have been filled using the priority order rules. See Appendix A.

Table 13

NS-SEC based on SOC2000 simplified and reduced derivation table: analytic classes

Standard Occupational Classification 2000 unit group	Simplified NS-SEC	Employment status				
		1 Employers	2 Self-employed - no employees	3 Managers	4 Supervisors	5 Other employees
1111 Senior officials in national government	1.1	1.1	1.1	1.1	1.1	1.1
1112 Directors and chief executives of major organisations	1.1	1.1	1.1	1.1	1.1	1.1
1113 Senior officials in local government	1.1	4	4	1.1	1.1	1.1
1114 Senior officials of special interest organisations	2	4	4	2	2	2
1121 Production, works and maintenance managers	1.1	4	4	1.1	1.1	1.1
1122 Managers in construction	2	4	4	2	2	2
1123 Managers in mining and energy	1.1	4	4	1.1	1.1	1.1
1131 Financial managers and chartered secretaries	1.1	1.2	1.2	1.1	1.1	1.1
1132 Marketing and sales managers	1.1	4	4	1.1	1.1	1.1
1133 Purchasing managers	1.1	4	4	1.1	1.1	1.1
1134 Advertising and public relations managers	1.1	4	4	1.1	1.1	1.1
1135 Personnel, training and industrial relations managers	1.1	4	4	1.1	1.1	1.1
1136 Information and communication technology managers	1.1	4	4	1.1	1.1	1.1
1137 Research and development managers	1.1	1.2	1.2	1.1	1.1	1.1
1141 Quality assurance managers	2	4	4	2	2	2
1142 Customer care managers	2	4	4	2	2	2
1151 Financial institution managers	2	4	4	2	2	2
1152 Office managers	2	4	4	2	2	2
1161 Transport and distribution managers	2	4	4	2	2	2
1162 Storage and warehouse managers	2	4	4	2	2	2
1163 Retail and wholesale managers	2	4	4	2	2	2
1171 Officers in armed forces	1.1	1.1	1.1	1.1	1.1	1.1
1172 Police officers (inspectors and above)	1.1	1.1	1.1	1.1	1.1	1.1
1173 Senior officers in fire, ambulance, prison and related services	1.1	1.1	1.1	1.1	1.1	1.1
1174 Security managers	2	4	4	2	2	2
1181 Hospital and health service managers	1.1	4	4	1.1	1.1	1.1
1182 Pharmacy managers	2	1.2	1.2	2	2	2
1183 Healthcare practice managers	2	4	4	2	2	2
1184 Social services managers	1.1	4	4	1.1	1.1	1.1
1185 Residential and day care managers	2	4	4	2	2	2
1211 Farm managers	2	4	4	2	2	2
1212 Natural environment and conservation managers	1.1	4	4	1.1	1.1	1.1
1219 Managers in animal husbandry, forestry and fishing n.e.c.	4	4	4	2	2	2
1221 Hotel and accommodation managers	4	4	4	2	2	2
1222 Conference and exhibition managers	2	4	4	2	2	2
1223 Restaurant and catering managers	4	4	4	2	2	2
1224 Publicans and managers of licensed premises	2	4	4	2	2	2
1225 Leisure and sports managers	2	4	4	2	2	2
1226 Travel agency managers	2	4	4	2	2	2
1231 Property, housing and land managers	1.1	4	4	1.1	1.1	1.1
1232 Garage managers and proprietors	4	4	4	2	2	2
1233 Hairdressing and beauty salon managers and proprietors	4	4	4	2	2	2
1234 Shopkeepers and wholesale/retail dealers	4	4	4	2	2	2
1235 Recycling and refuse disposal managers	2	4	4	2	2	2
1239 Managers and proprietors in other services n.e.c.	2	4	4	2	2	2
2111 Chemists	1.2	1.2	1.2	1.2	1.2	1.2
2112 Biological scientists and biochemists	1.2	1.2	1.2	1.2	1.2	1.2
2113 Physicists, geologists and meteorologists	1.2	1.2	1.2	1.2	1.2	1.2
2121 Civil engineers	1.2	1.2	1.2	1.2	1.2	1.2
2122 Mechanical engineers	1.2	1.2	1.2	1.2	1.2	1.2
2123 Electrical engineers	1.2	1.2	1.2	1.2	1.2	1.2
2124 Electronics engineers	1.2	1.2	1.2	1.2	1.2	1.2
2125 Chemical engineers	1.2	1.2	1.2	1.2	1.2	1.2
2126 Design and development engineers	1.2	1.2	1.2	1.2	1.2	1.2
2127 Production and process engineers	2	2	2	2	2	2
2128 Planning and quality control engineers	2	2	2	2	2	2
2129 Engineering professionals n.e.c.	1.2	1.2	1.2	1.2	1.2	1.2
2131 IT strategy and planning professionals	1.2	1.2	1.2	1.2	1.2	1.2

Please note: This derivation table has no empty cells. The shaded cells have been filled using the priority order rules. See Appendix A.

Table 13 - *continued*

Standard Occupational Classification 2000 unit group		Simplified NS-SEC	Employment status				
			1 Employers	2 Self-employed - no employees	3 Managers	4 Supervisors	5 Other employees
2132	Software professionals	1.2	1.2	1.2	1.2	1.2	1.2
2211	Medical practitioners	1.2	1.2	1.2	1.2	1.2	1.2
2212	Psychologists	1.2	1.2	1.2	1.2	1.2	1.2
2213	Pharmacists/pharmacologists	1.2	1.2	1.2	1.2	1.2	1.2
2214	Ophthalmic opticians	2	2	2	2	2	2
2215	Dental practitioners	1.2	1.2	1.2	1.2	1.2	1.2
2216	Veterinarians	1.2	1.2	1.2	1.2	1.2	1.2
2311	Higher education teaching professionals	1.2	1.2	1.2	1.2	1.2	1.2
2312	Further education teaching professionals	2	2	2	2	2	2
2313	Education officers, school inspectors	1.2	1.2	1.2	1.2	1.2	1.2
2314	Secondary education teaching professionals	2	2	2	2	2	2
2315	Primary and nursery education teaching professionals	2	2	2	2	2	2
2316	Special needs education teaching professionals	2	2	2	2	2	2
2317	Registrars and senior administrators of educational establishments	1.2	1.2	1.2	1.2	1.2	1.2
2319	Teaching professionals n.e.c.	4	4	4	3	2	3
2321	Scientific researchers	1.2	1.2	1.2	1.2	1.2	1.2
2322	Social science researchers	1.2	1.2	1.2	1.2	1.2	1.2
2329	Researchers n.e.c.	1.2	1.2	1.2	1.2	1.2	1.2
2411	Solicitors and lawyers, judges and coroners	1.2	1.2	1.2	1.2	1.2	1.2
2419	Legal professionals n.e.c.	1.2	1.2	1.2	1.2	1.2	1.2
2421	Chartered and certified accountants	1.2	1.2	1.2	1.2	1.2	1.2
2422	Management accountants	1.2	1.2	1.2	1.2	1.2	1.2
2423	Management consultants, actuaries, economists and statisticians	1.2	1.2	1.2	1.2	1.2	1.2
2431	Architects	1.2	1.2	1.2	1.2	1.2	1.2
2432	Town planners	1.2	1.2	1.2	1.2	1.2	1.2
2433	Quantity surveyors	2	2	2	2	2	2
2434	Chartered surveyors (not quantity surveyors)	1.2	1.2	1.2	1.2	1.2	1.2
2441	Public service administrative professionals	2	2	2	2	2	2
2442	Social workers	2	2	2	2	2	2
2443	Probation officers	1.2	1.2	1.2	1.2	1.2	1.2
2444	Clergy	1.2	1.2	1.2	1.2	1.2	1.2
2451	Librarians	2	2	2	2	2	2
2452	Archivists and curators	2	2	2	2	2	2
3111	Laboratory technicians	2	2	2	2	2	2
3112	Electrical/electronics technicians	3	4	4	3	2	3
3113	Engineering technicians	2	2	2	2	2	2
3114	Building and civil engineering technicians	2	2	2	2	2	2
3115	Quality assurance technicians	5	4	4	5	5	5
3119	Science and engineering technicians n.e.c.	2	2	2	2	2	2
3121	Architectural technologists and town planning technicians	2	2	2	2	2	2
3122	Draughtspersons	3	4	4	3	2	3
3123	Building inspectors	2	2	2	2	2	2
3131	IT operations technicians	2	2	2	2	2	2
3132	IT user support technicians	2	2	2	2	2	2
3211	Nurses	2	2	2	2	2	2
3212	Midwives	2	2	2	2	2	2
3213	Paramedics	2	2	3	3	2	3
3214	Medical radiographers	2	2	2	2	2	2
3215	Chiropodists	2	2	2	2	2	2
3216	Dispensing opticians	3	4	4	3	2	3
3217	Pharmaceutical dispensers	6	4	4	6	5	6
3218	Medical and dental technicians	3	4	4	3	2	3
3221	Physiotherapists	2	2	2	2	2	2
3222	Occupational therapists	2	2	2	2	2	2
3223	Speech and language therapists	1.2	1.2	1.2	1.2	1.2	1.2
3229	Therapists n.e.c.	2	2	2	2	2	2
3231	Youth and community workers	2	2	2	2	2	2
3232	Housing and welfare officers	2	2	2	2	2	2
3311	NCOs and other ranks	3	2	3	3	2	3
3312	Police officers (sergeant and below)	3	2	3	3	2	3
3313	Fire service officers (leading fire officer and below)	3	2	3	3	2	3
3314	Prison service officers (below principal officer)	3	2	3	3	2	3
3319	Protective service associate professionals n.e.c.	2	2	2	2	2	2
3411	Artists	2	2	2	2	2	2
3412	Authors, writers	2	2	2	2	2	2
3413	Actors, entertainers	2	2	2	2	2	2
3414	Dancers and choreographers	2	2	2	2	2	2
3415	Musicians	2	2	2	2	2	2

Please note: This derivation table has no empty cells. The shaded cells have been filled using the priority order rules. See Appendix A.
| *Indicates a change to the original shading. This does not affect the values in the cells.*

Table 13 - *continued*

Standard Occupational Classification 2000 unit group		Simplified NS-SEC	Employment status				
			1 Employers	2 Self-employed - no employees	3 Managers	4 Supervisors	5 Other employees
3416	Arts officers, producers and directors	2	2	2	2	2	2
3421	Graphic designers	3	4	4	3	2	3
3422	Product, clothing and related designers	4	4	4	3	2	3
3431	Journalists, newspaper and periodical editors	2	2	2	2	2	2
3432	Broadcasting associate professionals	2	2	2	2	2	2
3433	Public relations officers	2	2	2	2	2	2
3434	Photographers and audio-visual equipment operators	3	4	4	3	2	3
3441	Sports players	2	2	2	2	2	2
3442	Sports coaches, instructors and officials	2	2	2	2	2	2
3443	Fitness instructors	6	4	4	6	5	6
3449	Sports and fitness occupations n.e.c.	3	4	4	3	2	3
3511	Air traffic controllers	2	2	2	2	2	2
3512	Aircraft pilots and flight engineers	1.2	1.2	1.2	1.2	1.2	1.2
3513	Ship and hovercraft officers	2	2	2	2	2	2
3514	Train drivers	5	5	5	5	5	5
3520	Legal associate professionals	3	4	4	3	2	3
3531	Estimators, valuers and assessors	2	2	2	2	2	2
3532	Brokers	1.2	1.2	1.2	1.2	1.2	1.2
3533	Insurance underwriters	1.2	1.2	1.2	1.2	1.2	1.2
3534	Finance and investment analysts/advisers	2	2	2	2	2	2
3535	Taxation experts	1.2	1.2	1.2	1.2	1.2	1.2
3536	Importers, exporters	2	2	2	2	2	2
3537	Financial and accounting technicians	2	2	2	2	2	2
3539	Business and related associate professionals n.e.c.	2	2	2	2	2	2
3541	Buyers and purchasing officers	2	2	2	2	2	2
3542	Sales representatives	2	2	2	2	2	2
3543	Marketing associate professionals	2	2	2	2	2	2
3544	Estate agents, auctioneers	2	2	2	2	2	2
3551	Conservation and environmental protection officers	1.2	1.2	1.2	1.2	1.2	1.2
3552	Countryside and park rangers	3	4	4	3	2	3
3561	Public service associate professionals	2	2	2	2	2	2
3562	Personnel and industrial relations officers	2	2	2	2	2	2
3563	Vocational and industrial trainers and instructors	2	2	2	2	2	2
3564	Careers advisers and vocational guidance specialists	2	2	2	2	2	2
3565	Inspectors of factories, utilities and trading standards	2	2	2	2	2	2
3566	Statutory examiners	2	2	2	2	2	2
3567	Occupational hygienists and safety officers (health and safety)	2	2	2	2	2	2
3568	Environmental health officers	1.2	1.2	1.2	1.2	1.2	1.2
4111	Civil Service executive officers	2	2	2	2	2	2
4112	Civil Service administrative officers and assistants	3	2	3	3	2	3
4113	Local government clerical officers and assistants	3	2	3	3	2	3
4114	Officers of non-governmental organisations	2	2	2	2	2	2
4121	Credit controllers	3	4	4	3	2	3
4122	Accounts and wages clerks, book-keepers, other financial clerks	3	4	4	3	2	3
4123	Counter clerks	3	4	4	3	2	3
4131	Filing and other records assistants/clerks	3	4	4	3	2	3
4132	Pensions and insurance clerks	3	4	4	3	2	3
4133	Stock control clerks	6	4	4	6	5	6
4134	Transport and distribution clerks	3	4	4	3	2	3
4135	Library assistants/clerks	3	4	4	3	2	3
4136	Database assistants/clerks	3	4	4	3	2	3
4137	Market research interviewers	6	4	4	6	5	6
4141	Telephonists	6	4	4	6	5	6
4142	Communication operators	5	4	4	5	5	5
4150	General office assistants/clerks	3	4	4	3	2	3
4211	Medical secretaries	3	4	4	3	2	3
4212	Legal secretaries	3	4	4	3	2	3
4213	School secretaries	3	4	4	3	2	3
4214	Company secretaries	3	4	4	3	2	3
4215	Personal assistants and other secretaries	3	4	4	3	2	3
4216	Receptionists	6	4	4	6	5	6
4217	Typists	3	4	4	3	2	3
5111	Farmers	4	4	4	2	2	2
5112	Horticultural trades	6	4	4	6	5	6

Please note: This derivation table has no empty cells. The shaded cells have been filled using the priority order rules. See Appendix A.

Table 13 - *continued*

Standard Occupational Classification 2000 unit group	Simplified NS-SEC	Employment status				
		1 Employers	2 Self-employed - no employees	3 Managers	4 Supervisors	5 Other employees
5113 Gardeners and groundsmen/groundswomen	5	4	4	5	5	5
5119 Agricultural and fishing trades n.e.c.	4	4	4	5	5	5
5211 Smiths and forge workers	7	4	4	7	5	7
5212 Moulders, core makers, die casters	6	4	4	6	5	6
5213 Sheet metal workers	6	4	4	6	5	6
5214 Metal plate workers, shipwrights, riveters	7	4	4	7	5	7
5215 Welding trades	7	4	4	7	5	7
5216 Pipe fitters	7	4	4	7	5	7
5221 Metal machining setters and setter-operators	6	4	4	6	5	6
5222 Tool makers, tool fitters and markers-out	5	4	4	5	5	5
5223 Metal working production and maintenance fitters	5	4	4	5	5	5
5224 Precision instrument makers and repairers	5	4	4	5	5	5
5231 Motor mechanics, auto engineers	5	4	4	5	5	5
5232 Vehicle body builders and repairers	5	4	4	5	5	5
5233 Auto electricians	5	4	4	5	5	5
5234 Vehicle spray painters	6	4	4	6	5	6
5241 Electricians, electrical fitters	5	4	4	5	5	5
5242 Telecommunications engineers	3	4	4	3	2	3
5243 Lines repairers and cable jointers	5	4	4	5	5	5
5244 TV, video and audio engineers	5	4	4	5	5	5
5245 Computer engineers, installation and maintenance	3	4	4	3	2	3
5249 Electrical/electronics engineers n.e.c.	3	4	4	3	2	3
5311 Steel erectors	6	4	4	6	5	6
5312 Bricklayers, masons	4	4	4	7	5	7
5313 Roofers, roof tilers and slaters	4	4	4	7	5	7
5314 Plumbers, heating and ventilating engineers	5	4	4	5	5	5
5315 Carpenters and joiners	4	4	4	7	5	7
5316 Glaziers, window fabricators and fitters	4	4	4	7	5	7
5319 Construction trades n.e.c.	4	4	4	6	5	6
5321 Plasterers	4	4	4	7	5	7
5322 Floorers and wall tilers	4	4	4	7	5	7
5323 Painters and decorators	4	4	4	7	5	7
5411 Weavers and knitters	7	4	4	7	5	7
5412 Upholsterers	7	4	4	7	5	7
5413 Leather and related trades	7	4	4	7	5	7
5414 Tailors and dressmakers	6	4	4	6	5	6
5419 Textiles, garments and related trades n.e.c.	7	4	4	7	5	7
5421 Originators, compositors and print preparers	5	4	4	5	5	5
5422 Printers	5	4	4	5	5	5
5423 Bookbinders and print finishers	7	4	4	7	5	7
5424 Screen printers	5	4	4	5	5	5
5431 Butchers, meat cutters	7	4	4	7	5	7
5432 Bakers, flour confectioners	5	4	4	5	5	5
5433 Fishmongers, poultry dressers	7	4	4	7	5	7
5434 Chefs, cooks	6	4	4	6	5	6
5491 Glass and ceramics makers, decorators and finishers	7	4	4	7	5	7
5492 Furniture makers, other craft woodworkers	7	4	4	7	5	7
5493 Pattern makers (moulds)	5	4	4	5	5	5
5494 Musical instrument makers and tuners	4	4	4	5	5	5
5495 Goldsmiths, silversmiths, precious stone workers	5	4	4	5	5	5
5496 Floral arrangers, florists	7	4	4	7	5	7
5499 Hand craft occupations n.e.c.	5	4	4	5	5	5
6111 Nursing auxiliaries and assistants	3	4	4	3	2	3
6112 Ambulance staff (excluding paramedics)	3	2	3	3	2	3
6113 Dental nurses	6	4	4	6	5	6
6114 Houseparents and residential wardens	6	4	4	6	5	6
6115 Care assistants and home carers	6	4	4	6	5	6
6121 Nursery nurses	3	4	4	3	2	3
6122 Childminders and related occupations	4	4	4	7	5	7
6123 Playgroup leaders/assistants	6	4	4	6	5	6
6124 Educational assistants	6	4	4	6	5	6
6131 Veterinary nurses and assistants	6	4	4	6	5	6
6139 Animal care occupations n.e.c.	7	4	4	7	5	7
6211 Sports and leisure assistants	6	4	4	6	5	6
6212 Travel agents	3	4	4	3	2	3
6213 Travel and tour guides	7	4	4	7	5	7
6214 Air travel assistants	3	4	4	3	2	3
6215 Rail travel assistants	3	4	4	3	2	3
6219 Leisure and travel service occupations n.e.c.	7	4	4	7	5	7
6221 Hairdressers, barbers	7	4	4	7	5	7

Please note: This derivation table has no empty cells. The shaded cells have been filled using the priority order rules. See Appendix A.

Table 13 - *continued*

Standard Occupational Classification 2000 unit group		Simplified NS-SEC	Employment status				
			1 Employers	2 Self-employed - no employees	3 Managers	4 Supervisors	5 Other employees
6222	Beauticians and related occupations	4	4	4	6	5	6
6231	Housekeepers and related occupations	6	4	4	6	5	6
6232	Caretakers	6	4	4	6	5	6
6291	Undertakers and mortuary assistants	6	4	4	6	5	6
6292	Pest control officers	6	4	4	6	5	6
7111	Sales and retail assistants	6	4	4	6	5	6
7112	Retail cashiers and check-out operators	6	4	4	6	5	6
7113	Telephone salespersons	6	4	4	6	5	6
7121	Collector salespersons and credit agents	6	4	4	6	5	6
7122	Debt, rent and other cash collectors	3	4	4	3	2	3
7123	Roundsmen/women and van salespersons	7	4	4	7	5	7
7124	Market and street traders and assistants	4	4	4	7	5	7
7125	Merchandisers and window dressers	3	4	4	3	2	3
7129	Sales related occupations n.e.c.	3	4	4	3	2	3
7211	Call centre agents/operators	3	4	4	3	2	3
7212	Customer care occupations	3	4	4	3	2	3
8111	Food, drink and tobacco process operatives	6	4	4	6	5	6
8112	Glass and ceramics process operatives	6	4	4	6	5	6
8113	Textile process operatives	7	4	4	7	5	7
8114	Chemical and related process operatives	5	4	4	5	5	5
8115	Rubber process operatives	6	4	4	6	5	6
8116	Plastics process operatives	6	4	4	6	5	6
8117	Metal making and treating process operatives	6	4	4	6	5	6
8118	Electroplaters	6	4	4	6	5	6
8119	Process operatives n.e.c.	6	4	4	6	5	6
8121	Paper and wood machine operatives	6	4	4	6	5	6
8122	Coal mine operatives	7	4	4	7	5	7
8123	Quarry workers and related operatives	5	4	4	5	5	5
8124	Energy plant operatives	6	4	4	6	5	6
8125	Metal working machine operatives	6	4	4	6	5	6
8126	Water and sewerage plant operatives	5	4	4	5	5	5
8129	Plant and machine operatives n.e.c.	6	4	4	6	5	6
8131	Assemblers (electrical products)	6	4	4	6	5	6
8132	Assemblers (vehicles and metal goods)	6	4	4	6	5	6
8133	Routine inspectors and testers	5	4	4	5	5	5
8134	Weighers, graders, sorters	7	4	4	7	5	7
8135	Tyre, exhaust and windscreen fitters	6	4	4	6	5	6
8136	Clothing cutters	6	4	4	6	5	6
8137	Sewing machinists	7	4	4	7	5	7
8138	Routine laboratory testers	3	4	4	3	2	3
8139	Assemblers and routine operatives n.e.c.	7	4	4	7	5	7
8141	Scaffolders, stagers, riggers	6	4	4	6	5	6
8142	Road construction operatives	5	4	4	6	5	6
8143	Rail construction and maintenance operatives	5	4	4	5	5	5
8149	Construction operatives n.e.c.	5	4	4	7	5	7
8211	Heavy goods vehicle drivers	7	4	4	7	5	7
8212	Van drivers	7	4	4	7	5	7
8213	Bus and coach drivers	7	4	4	7	5	7
8214	Taxi, cab drivers and chauffeurs	4	4	4	7	5	7
8215	Driving instructors	4	4	4	6	5	6
8216	Rail transport operatives	5	4	4	5	5	5
8217	Seafarers (merchant navy); barge, lighter and boat operatives	6	4	4	6	5	6
8218	Air transport operatives	5	4	4	5	5	5
8219	Transport operatives n.e.c.	5	4	4	5	5	5
8221	Crane drivers	6	4	4	6	5	6
8222	Fork-lift truck drivers	6	4	4	6	5	6
8223	Agricultural machinery drivers	6	4	4	6	5	6
8229	Mobile machine drivers and operatives n.e.c.	7	4	4	7	5	7
9111	Farm workers	6	4	4	6	5	6
9112	Forestry workers	4	4	4	6	5	6
9119	Fishing and agriculture related occupations n.e.c.	7	4	4	7	5	7
9121	Labourers in building and woodworking trades	7	4	4	7	5	7
9129	Labourers in other construction trades n.e.c.	7	4	4	7	5	7
9131	Labourers in foundries	7	4	4	7	5	7
9132	Industrial cleaning process occupations	7	4	4	7	5	7
9133	Printing machine minders and assistants	6	4	4	6	5	6
9134	Packers, bottlers, canners, fillers	7	4	4	7	5	7
9139	Labourers in process and plant operations n.e.c.	7	4	4	7	5	7
9141	Stevedores, dockers and slingers	7	4	4	7	5	7
9149	Other goods handling and storage occupations n.e.c.	7	4	4	7	5	7

Please note: This derivation table has no empty cells. The shaded cells have been filled using the priority order rules. See Appendix A.

Table 13 - *continued*

Standard Occupational Classification 2000 unit group		Simplified NS-SEC	Employment status				
			1 Employers	2 Self-employed - no employees	3 Managers	4 Supervisors	5 Other employees
9211	Postal workers, mail sorters, messengers, couriers	6	4	4	6	5	6
9219	Elementary office occupations n.e.c.	6	4	4	6	5	6
9221	Hospital porters	6	4	4	6	5	6
9222	Hotel porters	7	4	4	7	5	7
9223	Kitchen and catering assistants	6	4	4	6	5	6
9224	Waiters, waitresses	7	4	4	7	5	7
9225	Bar staff	7	4	4	7	5	7
9226	Leisure and theme park attendants	7	4	4	7	5	7
9229	Elementary personal services occupations n.e.c.	7	4	4	7	5	7
9231	Window cleaners	4	4	4	7	5	7
9232	Road sweepers	7	4	4	7	5	7
9233	Cleaners, domestics	7	4	4	7	5	7
9234	Launderers, dry cleaners, pressers	7	4	4	7	5	7
9235	Refuse and salvage occupations	7	4	4	7	5	7
9239	Elementary cleaning occupations n.e.c.	7	4	4	7	5	7
|9241	Security guards and related occupations	6	4	4	6	5	6
9242	Traffic wardens	6	5	6	6	5	6
9243	School crossing patrol attendants	7	5	7	7	5	7
|9244	School mid-day assistants	7	5	7	7	5	7
9245	Car park attendants	7	4	4	7	5	7
9249	Elementary security occupations n.e.c.	6	4	4	6	5	6
9251	Shelf fillers	6	4	4	6	5	6
9259	Elementary sales occupations n.e.c.	6	4	4	6	5	6

Please note: This derivation table has no empty cells. The shaded cells have been filled using the priority order rules. See Appendix A.
| Indicates a change to the original shading. This does not affect the values in the cells.

17 NS-SEC derivation tables based on SOC90

Table **14**

NS-SEC based on SOC90 simplified and full derivation table: operational categories

Standard Occupational Classification 990 unit group		Simplified NS-SEC	Employment status/size of organisation						
			1 Employers - large organisations	2 Employers - small organisations	3 Self-employed - no employees	4 Managers - large organisations	5 Managers - small organisations	6 Supervisors	7 Other employees
100	General administrators; national government (Assistant Secretary/ Grade 5 and above)	2	2	2	2	2	2	2	2
101	General managers; large companies and organisations	2	1	1	1	2	2	2	2
102	Local government officers (administrative and executive functions)	2	9.1	9.1	9.1	2	2	2	2
103	General administrators; national government (HEO to Senior Principal/Grade 6)	4.1	4.1	4.1	4.1	4.1	4.1	4.1	4.1
110	Production, works and maintenance managers	2	1	8.1	9.1	2	5	6	5
111	Managers in building and contracting	5	1	8.1	9.1	5	5	5	5
112	Clerks of works	5	1	8.1	9.1	5	5	5	5
113	Managers in mining and energy industries	2	1	8.1	9.1	2	5	5	5
120	Treasurers and company financial managers	2	3.3	3.3	3.3	2	2	2	2
121	Marketing and sales managers	2	1	8.1	4.3	2	5	5	5
122	Purchasing managers	2	1	8.1	9.1	2	5	5	5
123	Advertising and public relations managers	2	1	8.1	4.3	2	5	5	5
124	Personnel, training and industrial relations managers	2	1	8.1	9.1	2	4.1	4.1	4.1
125	Organisation and methods and work study managers	2	1	8.1	9.1	2	5	5	5
126	Computer systems and data processing managers	2	1	8.1	9.1	2	5	5	5
127	Company secretaries	7.1	1	8.1	9.1	7.1	7.1	6	7.1
130	Credit controllers	7.1	1	8.1	9.1	7.1	7.1	6	7.1
131	Bank, Building Society and Post Office managers (except self-employed)	5	1	8.1	9.1	5	5	5	5
132	Civil Service executive officers	4.1	4.1	4.1	4.1	4.1	4.1	4.1	4.1
139	Other financial institution and office managers n.e.c.	5	1	8.1	9.1	5	5	5	5
140	Transport managers	5	1	8.1	9.1	5	5	5	5
141	Stores controllers	12.6	1	8.1	9.1	12.6	5	5	5
142	Managers in warehousing and other materials handling	5	1	8.1	9.1	5	5	5	5
150	Officers in UK armed forces	2	2	2	2	2	2	2	2
151	Officers in foreign and Commonwealth armed forces	2	2	2	2	2	2	2	2
152	Police officers (inspector and above)	2	2	2	2	2	2	2	2
153	Fire service officers (station officer and above)	2	2	2	2	2	2	2	2
154	Prison officers (principal officer and above)	2	2	2	2	2	2	2	2
155	Customs and excise, immigration service officers (customs: chief preventive officer and above; excise: surveyor and above)	2	2	2	2	2	2	2	2
160	Farm owners and managers, horticulturists	9.2	1	8.2	9.2	5	5	6	5
169	Other managers in farming, horticulture, forestry and fishing n.e.c.	9.2	1	8.2	9.2	11.1	5	5	5
170	Property and estate managers	5	1	8.1	9.1	2	5	5	5
171	Garage managers and proprietors	8.1	1	8.1	9.1	5	5	5	5
172	Hairdressers' and barbers' managers and proprietors	9.1	1	8.1	9.1	5	5	5	5
173	Hotel and accommodation managers	9.1	1	8.1	9.1	5	5	5	5
174	Restaurant and catering managers	5	1	8.1	9.1	5	5	5	5
175	Publicans, innkeepers and club stewards	5	1	8.1	9.1	5	5	5	5

Please note: This derivation table has no empty cells. See key at end of table.

Table 14 - *continued*

Standard Occupational Classification 1990 unit group		Simplified NS-SEC	Employment status/size of organisation						
			1 Employers - large organisations	2 Employers - small organisations	3 Self-employed - no employees	4 Managers - large organisations	5 Managers - small organisations	6 Supervisors	7 Other employees
176	Entertainment and sports managers	5	1	8.1	9.1	5	5	5	5
177	Travel agency managers	5	1	8.1	9.1	5	5	5	5
178	Managers and proprietors of butchers and fishmongers	8.1	1	8.1	9.1	5	5	5	5
179	Managers and proprietors in service industries n.e.c.	5	1	8.1	9.1	5	5	5	5
190	Officials of trade associations, trade unions, professional bodies and charities	4.1	1	8.1	9.1	2	5	4.1	4.1
191	Registrars and administrators of educational establishments	3.1	3.1	3.1	3.1	3.1	3.1	3.1	3.1
199	Other managers and administrators n.e.c.	5	1	8.1	9.1	5	5	5	5
200	Chemists	3.1	3.3	3.3	3.3	2	5	3.1	3.1
201	Biological scientists and biochemists	3.1	3.3	3.3	3.3	2	5	3.1	3.1
202	Physicists, geologists and meteorologists	3.1	3.3	3.3	3.3	2	5	3.1	3.1
209	Other natural scientists n.e.c.	3.1	3.3	3.3	3.3	3.1	3.1	3.1	3.1
210	Civil, structural, municipal, mining and quarrying engineers	3.1	3.3	3.3	3.3	3.1	3.1	3.1	3.1
211	Mechanical engineers	3.1	3.3	3.3	3.3	3.1	3.1	3.1	3.1
212	Electrical engineers	3.1	3.3	3.3	3.3	3.1	3.1	3.1	3.1
213	Electronic engineers	3.1	3.3	3.3	3.3	3.1	3.1	3.1	3.1
214	Software engineers	3.1	3.3	3.3	3.3	3.1	3.1	3.1	3.1
215	Chemical engineers	3.1	3.3	3.3	3.3	3.1	3.1	3.1	3.1
216	Design and development engineers	3.1	3.3	3.3	3.3	3.1	3.1	3.1	3.1
217	Process and production engineers	4.1	1	4.3	4.3	4.1	4.1	4.1	4.1
218	Planning and quality control engineers	4.1	1	4.3	4.3	5	5	4.1	4.1
219	Other engineers and technologists n.e.c.	3.1	3.3	3.3	3.3	3.1	3.1	3.1	3.1
220	Medical practitioners	3.1	3.3	3.3	3.3	3.1	3.1	3.1	3.1
221	Pharmacists/pharmacologists	3.1	3.3	3.3	3.3	2	5	3.1	3.1
222	Ophthalmic opticians	4.1	1	4.3	4.3	4.1	4.1	4.1	4.1
223	Dental practitioners	3.3	3.3	3.3	3.3	3.1	3.1	3.1	3.1
224	Veterinarians	3.1	3.3	3.3	3.3	3.1	3.1	3.1	3.1
230	University and polytechnic teaching professionals	3.1	3.3	3.3	3.3	3.1	3.1	3.1	3.1
231	Higher and further education teaching professionals	4.1	1	4.3	4.3	4.1	4.1	4.1	4.1
232	Education officers, school inspectors	3.1	3.1	3.1	3.1	3.1	3.1	3.1	3.1
233	Secondary (and middle school deemed secondary) education teaching professionals	4.1	1	4.3	4.3	4.1	4.1	4.1	4.1
234	Primary (and middle school deemed primary) and nursery education teaching professionals	4.1	1	4.3	4.3	4.1	4.1	4.1	4.1
235	Special education teaching professionals	4.1	1	4.3	4.3	4.1	4.1	4.1	4.1
239	Other teaching professionals n.e.c.	9.1	1	8.1	9.1	7.3	7.3	6	7.3
240	Judges and officers of the Court	3.1	3.3	3.3	3.3	3.1	3.1	3.1	3.1
241	Barristers and advocates	3.3	3.3	3.3	3.3	3.1	3.1	3.1	3.1
242	Solicitors	3.1	3.3	3.3	3.3	3.1	3.1	3.1	3.1
250	Chartered and certified accountants	3.1	3.3	3.3	3.3	3.1	3.1	3.1	3.1
251	Management accountants	3.2	3.4	3.4	3.4	3.2	3.2	3.2	3.2
252	Actuaries, economists and statisticians	3.1	3.3	3.3	3.3	3.1	3.1	3.1	3.1
253	Management consultants, business analysts	3.2	3.4	3.4	3.4	3.2	3.2	3.2	3.2
260	Architects	3.1	3.3	3.3	3.3	3.1	3.1	3.1	3.1
261	Town planners	3.1	3.3	3.3	3.3	3.1	3.1	3.1	3.1
262	Building, land, mining and 'general practice' surveyors	3.1	3.3	3.3	3.3	3.1	3.1	3.1	3.1
270	Librarians	4.1	4.3	4.3	4.3	4.1	4.1	4.1	4.1
271	Archivists and curators	4.1	4.3	4.3	4.3	4.1	4.1	4.1	4.1
290	Psychologists	3.1	3.3	3.3	3.3	3.1	3.1	3.1	3.1
291	Other social and behavioural scientists	3.1	3.3	3.3	3.3	3.1	3.1	3.1	3.1
292	Clergy	3.1	3.3	3.3	3.3	3.1	3.1	3.1	3.1
293	Social workers, probation officers	4.1	4.3	4.3	4.3	4.1	4.1	4.1	4.1
300	Laboratory technicians	4.1	1	4.3	4.3	4.1	4.1	4.1	4.1
301	Engineering technicians	4.1	1	4.3	4.3	4.1	4.1	4.1	4.1
302	Electrical/electronic technicians	7.3	1	8.1	9.1	7.3	7.3	6	7.3
303	Architectural and town planning technicians	4.1	1	4.3	4.3	4.1	4.1	4.1	4.1

Please note: This derivation table has no empty cells. See key at end of table.

Table 14 - *continued*

Standard Occupational Classification 1990 unit group		Simplified NS-SEC	Employment status/size of organisation						
			1 Employers - large organisations	2 Employers - small organisations	3 Self-employed - no employees	4 Managers - large organisations	5 Managers - small organisations	6 Supervisors	7 Other employees
304	Building and civil engineering technicians	4.1	1	4.3	4.3	4.1	4.1	4.1	4.1
309	Other scientific technicians n.e.c.	4.1	1	4.3	4.3	4.1	4.1	4.1	4.1
310	Draughtspersons	7.3	1	8.1	9.1	7.3	7.3	6	7.3
311	Building inspectors	4.1	4.3	4.3	4.3	4.1	4.1	4.1	4.1
312	Quantity surveyors	4.1	1	4.3	4.3	4.1	4.1	4.1	4.1
313	Marine, insurance and other surveyors	4.1	3.3	3.3	3.3	4.1	4.1	3.1	4.1
320	Computer analyst/programmers	3.2	3.4	3.4	3.4	3.2	3.2	3.2	3.2
330	Air traffic planners and controllers	4.1	4.1	4.1	4.1	4.1	4.1	4.1	4.1
331	Aircraft flight deck officers	3.2	3.4	3.4	3.4	3.2	3.2	3.2	3.2
332	Ship and hovercraft officers	4.1	1	4.3	4.3	4.1	4.1	4.1	4.1
340	Nurses	4.1	1	8.1	4.3	4.1	4.1	4.1	4.1
341	Midwives	4.1	1	4.3	4.3	4.1	4.1	4.1	4.1
342	Medical radiographers	4.1	1	4.3	4.3	4.1	4.1	4.1	4.1
343	Physiotherapists	4.1	1	4.3	4.3	4.1	4.1	4.1	4.1
344	Chiropodists	4.1	1	4.3	4.3	4.1	4.1	4.1	4.1
345	Dispensing opticians	7.3	1	8.1	9.1	7.3	7.3	6	7.3
346	Medical technicians, dental auxiliaries	12.1	1	8.1	9.1	7.3	7.3	10	12.1
347	Occupational and speech therapists, psychotherapists, therapists n.e.c.	4.1	1	4.3	4.3	4.1	4.1	4.1	4.1
348	Environmental health officers	3.2	3.2	3.2	3.2	3.2	3.2	3.2	3.2
349	Other health associate professionals n.e.c.	12.2	1	8.1	9.1	12.2	12.2	10	12.2
350	Legal service and related occupations	7.1	1	3.3	9.1	7.1	7.1	6	7.1
360	Estimators, valuers	4.1	1	4.3	4.3	4.1	4.1	4.1	4.1
361	Underwriters, claims assessors, brokers, investment analysts	4.1	1	4.3	4.3	3.2	4.1	4.1	4.1
362	Taxation experts	3.2	3.4	3.4	3.4	3.2	3.2	3.2	3.2
363	Personnel and industrial relations officers	4.1	1	4.3	4.3	4.1	4.1	4.1	4.1
364	Organisation and methods and work study officers	3.1	3.3	3.3	3.3	3.1	3.1	3.1	3.1
370	Matrons, houseparents	12.7	1	8.1	9.1	10	10	10	12.7
371	Welfare, community and youth workers	4.1	1	4.3	4.3	4.1	4.1	4.1	4.1
380	Authors, writers, journalists	4.1	1	4.3	4.3	4.1	4.1	4.1	4.1
381	Artists, commercial artists, graphic designers	9.1	1	8.1	9.1	7.3	7.3	6	7.3
382	Industrial designers	9.1	1	8.1	9.1	6	6	6	7.3
383	Clothing designers	7.3	1	8.1	9.1	6	6	6	7.3
384	Actors, entertainers, stage managers, producers and directors	4.3	1	4.3	4.3	4.1	4.1	4.1	4.1
385	Musicians	4.3	1	4.3	4.3	4.1	4.1	4.1	4.1
386	Photographers, camera, sound and video equipment operators	7.3	1	8.1	9.1	7.3	7.3	6	7.3
387	Professional athletes, sports officials	4.2	1	4.4	4.4	4.2	4.2	4.2	4.2
390	Information officers	4.1	1	4.3	4.3	4.1	4.1	4.1	4.1
391	Vocational and industrial trainers	4.1	1	4.3	4.3	4.1	4.1	4.1	4.1
392	Careers advisers and vocational guidance specialists	4.1	1	4.3	4.3	4.1	4.1	4.1	4.1
393	Driving instructors (excluding HGV)	9.1	1	8.1	9.1	12.2	12.2	10	12.2
394	Inspectors of factories, utilities and trading standards	4.1	4.1	4.1	4.1	4.1	4.1	4.1	4.1
395	Other statutory and similar inspectors n.e.c.	4.1	4.1	4.1	4.1	4.1	4.1	4.1	4.1
396	Occupational hygienists and safety officers (health and safety)	4.1	1	4.3	4.3	4.1	4.1	4.1	4.1
399	Other associate professional and technical occupations n.e.c.	4.1	1	4.3	4.3	2	5	4.1	4.1
400	Civil Service administrative officers and assistants	7.1	7.1	7.1	7.1	7.1	7.1	6	7.1
401	Local government clerical officers and assistants	7.1	7.1	7.1	7.1	7.1	7.1	6	7.1
410	Accounts and wages clerks, book-keepers, other financial clerks	7.1	1	8.1	9.1	7.1	7.1	6	7.1
411	Counter clerks and cashiers	7.1	1	8.1	9.1	7.1	7.1	6	7.1
412	Debt, rent and other cash collectors	7.2	1	8.1	9.1	7.2	7.2	6	7.2
420	Filing, computer and other records clerks (including legal conveyancing)	7.1	1	8.1	9.1	7.1	7.1	6	7.1
421	Library assistants/clerks	7.1	1	8.1	9.1	7.1	7.1	6	7.1
430	Clerks (n.o.s.)	7.2	1	8.1	9.1	7.2	7.2	6	7.2
440	Stores, despatch and production control clerks	12.6	1	8.1	9.1	12.6	12.6	10	12.6

Please note: This derivation table has no empty cells. See key at end of table.

Table 14 - *continued*

Standard Occupational Classification 1990 unit group		Simplified NS-SEC	Employment status/size of organisation						
			1 Employers - large organisations	2 Employers - small organisations	3 Self-employed - no employees	4 Managers - large organisations	5 Managers - small organisations	6 Supervisors	7 Other employees
441	Storekeepers and warehousemen/women	13.4	1	8.1	9.1	12.4	12.4	10	13.4
450	Medical secretaries	7.1	1	8.1	9.1	7.1	7.1	6	7.1
451	Legal secretaries	7.1	1	8.1	9.1	7.1	7.1	6	7.1
452	Typists and word processor operators	7.1	1	8.1	9.1	7.1	7.1	6	7.1
459	Other secretaries, personal assistants, typists, word processor operators n.e.c.	7.1	1	8.1	9.1	7.1	7.1	6	7.1
460	Receptionists	12.6	1	8.1	9.1	12.6	12.6	10	12.6
461	Receptionist/telephonists	12.6	1	8.1	9.1	12.6	12.6	10	12.6
462	Telephone operators	12.6	1	8.1	9.1	12.6	12.6	10	12.6
463	Radio and telegraph operators, other office communication system operators	11.1	1	8.1	9.1	11.1	11.1	10	11.1
490	Computer operators, data processing operators, other office machine operators	7.1	1	8.1	9.1	7.1	7.1	6	7.1
491	Tracers, drawing office assistants	7.3	1	8.1	9.1	7.3	7.3	6	7.3
500	Bricklayers, masons	9.1	1	8.1	9.1	13.3	13.3	10	13.3
501	Roofers, slaters, tilers, sheeters, cladders	9.1	1	8.1	9.1	13.2	13.2	10	13.2
502	Plasterers	9.1	1	8.1	9.1	13.3	13.3	10	13.3
503	Glaziers	13.2	1	8.1	9.1	13.2	13.2	10	13.2
504	Builders, building contractors	9.1	1	8.1	9.1	12.4	12.4	10	12.4
505	Scaffolders, stagers, steeplejacks, riggers	12.4	1	8.1	9.1	12.4	12.4	10	12.4
506	Floorers, floor coverers, carpet fitters and planners, floor and wall tilers	9.1	1	8.1	9.1	13.3	13.3	10	13.3
507	Painters and decorators	9.1	1	8.1	9.1	13.3	13.3	10	13.3
509	Other construction trades n.e.c.	9.1	1	8.1	9.1	12.4	12.4	10	12.4
510	Centre, capstan, turret and other lathe setters and setter-operators	12.3	1	8.1	9.1	12.3	12.3	10	12.3
511	Boring and drilling machine setters and setter-operators	12.3	1	8.1	9.1	12.3	12.3	10	12.3
512	Grinding machine setters and setter-operators	12.3	1	8.1	9.1	12.3	12.3	10	12.3
513	Milling machine setters and setter-operators	12.3	1	8.1	9.1	12.3	12.3	10	12.3
514	Press setters and setter-operators	10	1	8.1	9.1	12.3	12.3	10	12.3
515	Tool makers, tool fitters and markers-out	11.1	1	8.1	9.1	11.1	11.1	10	11.1
516	Metal working production and maintenance fitters	11.1	1	8.1	9.1	10	10	10	11.1
517	Precision instrument makers and repairers	11.1	1	8.1	9.1	11.1	11.1	10	11.1
518	Goldsmiths, silversmiths, precious stone workers	11.1	1	8.1	9.1	11.1	11.1	10	11.1
519	Other machine tool setters and setter-operators n.e.c. (including CNC setter-operators)	12.3	1	8.1	9.1	12.3	12.3	10	12.3
520	Production fitters (electrical/electronic)	11.1	1	8.1	9.1	11.1	11.1	10	11.1
521	Electricians, electrical maintenance fitters	11.1	1	8.1	9.1	11.1	11.1	10	11.1
522	Electrical engineers (not professional)	11.1	1	8.1	9.1	11.1	11.1	10	11.1
523	Telephone fitters	7.4	1	8.1	9.1	7.4	7.4	6	7.4
524	Cable jointers, lines repairers	11.1	1	8.1	9.1	11.1	11.1	10	11.1
525	Radio, TV and video engineers	11.1	1	8.1	9.1	11.1	11.1	10	11.1
526	Computer engineers, installation and maintenance	7.4	1	8.1	9.1	7.4	7.4	6	7.4
529	Other electrical/electronic trades n.e.c.	7.4	1	8.1	9.1	7.4	7.4	6	7.4
530	Smiths and forge workers	13.3	1	8.1	9.1	13.3	13.3	10	13.3
531	Moulders, core makers, die casters	12.3	1	8.1	9.1	12.3	12.3	10	12.3
532	Plumbers, heating and ventilating engineers and related trades	11.1	1	8.1	9.1	10	10	10	11.1
533	Sheet metal workers	12.3	1	8.1	9.1	12.3	12.3	10	12.3
534	Metal plate workers, shipwrights, riveters	13.3	1	8.1	9.1	13.3	13.3	10	13.3
535	Steel erectors	12.3	1	8.1	9.1	12.3	12.3	10	12.3
536	Barbenders, steel fixers	9.1	1	8.1	9.1	12.4	12.4	10	12.4
537	Welding trades	13.3	1	8.1	9.1	13.3	13.3	10	13.3
540	Motor mechanics, auto engineers (including road patrol engineers)	11.1	1	8.1	9.1	11.1	11.1	10	11.1
541	Coach and vehicle body builders	11.1	1	8.1	9.1	11.1	11.1	10	11.1

Please note: This derivation table has no empty cells. See key at end of table.

Table 14 - *continued*

Standard Occupational Classification 1990 unit group		Simplified NS-SEC	Employment status/size of organisation						
			1 Employers - large organisations	2 Employers - small organisations	3 Self-employed - no employees	4 Managers - large organisations	5 Managers - small organisations	6 Supervisors	7 Other employees
542	Vehicle body repairers, panel beaters	11.1	1	8.1	9.1	11.1	11.1	10	11.1
543	Auto electricians	11.1	1	8.1	9.1	11.1	11.1	10	11.1
544	Tyre and exhaust fitters	12.4	1	8.1	9.1	12.4	12.4	10	12.4
550	Weavers	13.3	1	8.1	9.1	13.3	13.3	10	13.3
551	Knitters	13.3	1	8.1	9.1	13.3	13.3	10	13.3
552	Warp preparers, bleachers, dyers and finishers	13.2	1	8.1	9.1	13.2	13.2	10	13.2
553	Sewing machinists, menders, darners and embroiderers	13.2	1	8.1	9.1	13.2	13.2	10	13.2
554	Coach trimmers, upholsterers and mattress makers	13.3	1	8.1	9.1	13.3	13.3	10	13.3
555	Shoe repairers, leather cutters and sewers, footwear lasters, makers and finishers, other leather making and repairing	13.3	1	8.1	9.1	13.3	13.3	10	13.3
556	Tailors and dressmakers	9.1	1	8.1	9.1	12.3	12.3	10	12.3
557	Clothing cutters, milliners, furriers	12.3	1	8.1	9.1	12.3	12.3	10	12.3
559	Other textiles, garments and related trades n.e.c.	13.3	1	8.1	9.1	13.3	13.3	10	13.3
560	Originators, compositors and print preparers	11.1	1	8.1	9.1	11.1	11.1	10	11.1
561	Printers	11.1	1	8.1	9.1	11.1	11.1	10	11.1
562	Bookbinders and print finishers	13.3	1	8.1	9.1	13.3	13.3	10	13.3
563	Screen printers	11.1	1	8.1	9.1	11.1	11.1	10	11.1
569	Other printing and related trades n.e.c.	11.1	1	8.1	9.1	11.1	11.1	10	11.1
570	Carpenters and joiners	9.1	1	8.1	9.1	13.3	13.3	10	13.3
571	Cabinet makers	13.3	1	8.1	9.1	13.3	13.3	10	13.3
572	Case and box makers	12.3	1	8.1	9.1	12.3	12.3	10	12.3
573	Pattern makers (moulds)	11.1	1	8.1	9.1	11.1	11.1	10	11.1
579	Other woodworking trades n.e.c.	9.1	1	8.1	9.1	13.3	13.3	10	13.3
580	Bakers, flour confectioners	11.1	1	8.1	9.1	11.1	11.1	10	11.1
581	Butchers, meat cutters	13.3	1	8.1	9.1	13.3	13.3	10	13.3
582	Fishmongers, poultry dressers	13.3	1	8.1	9.1	13.3	13.3	10	13.3
590	Glass product and ceramics makers	13.3	1	8.1	9.1	13.3	13.3	10	13.3
591	Glass product and ceramics finishers and decorators	13.3	1	8.1	9.1	13.3	13.3	10	13.3
592	Dental technicians	7.3	1	8.1	9.1	7.3	7.3	6	7.3
593	Musical instrument makers, piano tuners	9.1	1	8.1	9.1	11.1	11.1	10	11.1
594	Gardeners, groundsmen/groundswomen	11.1	1	8.1	9.1	11.1	11.1	10	11.1
595	Horticultural trades	12.5	1	8.2	9.2	12.5	12.5	10	12.5
596	Coach painters, other spray painters	12.3	1	8.1	9.1	12.3	12.3	10	12.3
597	Face trained coalmining workers, shotfirers and deputies	13.3	1	8.1	9.1	13.3	13.3	10	13.3
598	Office machinery mechanics	7.4	1	8.1	9.1	7.4	7.4	6	7.4
599	Other craft and related occupations n.e.c.	11.1	1	8.1	9.1	11.1	11.1	10	11.1
600	NCOs and other ranks, UK armed forces	7.2	7.2	7.2	7.2	7.2	7.2	6	7.2
601	NCOs and other ranks, foreign and Commonwealth armed forces	7.2	7.2	7.2	7.2	7.2	7.2	6	7.2
610	Police officers (sergeant and below)	7.2	7.2	7.2	7.2	7.2	7.2	6	7.2
611	Fire service officers (leading fire officer and below)	7.2	7.2	7.2	7.2	7.2	7.2	6	7.2
612	Prison service officers (below principal officer)	7.2	7.2	7.2	7.2	7.2	7.2	6	7.2
613	Customs and excise officers, immigration officers (customs: below chief preventive officer; excise: below surveyor)	4.1	4.1	4.1	4.1	4.1	4.1	4.1	4.1
614	Traffic wardens	12.2	12.2	12.2	12.2	12.2	12.2	10	12.2
615	Security guards and related occupations	12.2	1	8.1	9.1	5	5	10	12.2
619	Other security and protective service occupations n.e.c.	13.1	1	8.1	9.1	13.1	13.1	10	13.1
620	Chefs, cooks	12.2	1	8.1	9.1	10	10	10	12.2
621	Waiters, waitresses	13.1	1	8.1	9.1	13.1	13.1	10	13.1
622	Bar staff	13.1	1	8.1	9.1	13.1	13.1	10	13.1
630	Travel and flight attendants	13.1	1	8.1	9.1	13.1	13.1	6	13.1
631	Railway station staff	11.2	1	8.1	9.1	11.2	11.2	10	11.2
640	Assistant nurses, nursing auxiliaries	7.3	1	8.1	9.1	7.3	7.3	6	7.3
641	Hospital ward assistants	7.3	1	8.1	9.1	7.3	7.3	6	7.3
642	Ambulance staff	7.2	7.2	7.2	7.2	7.2	7.2	6	7.2

Please note: This derivation table has no empty cells. See key at end of table.

Table 14 - *continued*

Standard Occupational Classification 1990 unit group		Simplified NS-SEC	Employment status/size of organisation						
			1 Employers - large organisations	2 Employers - small organisations	3 Self-employed - no employees	4 Managers - large organisations	5 Managers - small organisations	6 Supervisors	7 Other employees
643	Dental nurses	12.2	1	8.1	9.1	12.2	12.2	10	12.2
644	Care assistants and attendants	12.2	1	8.1	9.1	12.2	12.2	10	12.2
650	Nursery nurses	7.2	1	8.1	9.1	7.2	7.2	6	7.2
651	Playgroup leaders	12.7	1	8.1	9.1	12.7	12.7	10	12.7
652	Educational assistants	12.7	1	8.1	9.1	12.7	12.7	10	12.7
659	Other childcare and related occupations n.e.c.	13.1	1	8.1	9.1	13.1	13.1	10	13.1
660	Hairdressers, barbers	13.1	1	8.1	9.1	13.1	13.1	10	13.1
661	Beauticians and related occupations	9.1	1	8.1	9.1	12.2	12.2	10	12.2
670	Domestic housekeepers and related occupations	12.2	1	8.1	9.1	12.2	12.2	10	12.2
671	Housekeepers (non-domestic)	10	1	8.1	9.1	12.2	12.2	10	12.2
672	Caretakers	12.2	1	8.1	9.1	12.2	12.2	10	12.2
673	Launderers, dry cleaners, pressers	13.2	1	8.1	9.1	13.2	13.2	10	13.2
690	Undertakers	12.2	1	8.1	9.1	12.2	12.2	10	12.2
691	Bookmakers	5	1	8.1	9.1	5	5	10	12.2
699	Other personal and protective service occupations n.e.c.	12.2	1	8.1	9.1	12.2	12.2	10	12.2
700	Buyers (retail trade)	4.1	1	4.3	4.3	4.1	4.1	4.1	4.1
701	Buyers and purchasing officers (not retail)	4.1	1	4.3	4.3	4.1	4.1	4.1	4.1
702	Importers and exporters	4.2	1	4.4	4.4	4.2	4.2	4.2	4.2
703	Air, commodity and ship brokers	3.2	3.4	3.4	3.4	3.2	3.2	3.2	3.2
710	Technical and wholesale sales representatives	4.2	1	4.4	4.4	2	5	4.2	4.2
719	Other sales representatives n.e.c.	7.2	1	4.4	4.4	4.2	4.2	6	7.2
720	Sales assistants	12.1	1	8.1	9.1	12.1	12.1	10	12.1
721	Retail cash desk and check-out operators	12.1	1	8.1	9.1	12.1	12.1	10	12.1
722	Petrol pump forecourt attendants	12.1	1	8.1	9.1	12.1	12.1	10	12.1
730	Collector salespersons and credit agents	9.1	1	8.1	9.1	12.1	12.1	10	12.1
731	Roundsmen/women and van salespersons	13.3	1	8.1	9.1	13.3	13.3	10	13.3
732	Market and street traders and assistants	9.1	1	8.1	9.1	13.1	13.1	10	13.1
733	Scrap dealers, scrap metal merchants	9.1	1	8.1	9.1	5	5	5	5
790	Merchandisers	7.2	1	8.1	9.1	7.2	7.2	6	7.2
791	Window dressers, floral arrangers	13.1	1	8.1	9.1	13.1	13.1	10	13.1
792	Telephone salespersons	12.1	1	8.1	9.1	12.1	12.1	10	12.1
800	Bakery and confectionery process operatives	12.4	1	8.1	9.1	12.4	12.4	10	12.4
801	Brewery and vinery process operatives	12.4	1	8.1	9.1	12.4	12.4	10	12.4
802	Tobacco process operatives	12.4	1	8.1	9.1	12.4	12.4	10	12.4
809	Other food, drink and tobacco process operatives n.e.c.	12.4	1	8.1	9.1	12.4	12.4	10	12.4
810	Tannery production operatives	11.2	1	8.1	9.1	11.2	11.2	10	11.2
811	Preparatory fibre processors	13.2	1	8.1	9.1	13.2	13.2	10	13.2
812	Spinners, doublers, twisters	13.2	1	8.1	9.1	13.2	13.2	10	13.2
813	Winders, reelers	13.2	1	8.1	9.1	13.2	13.2	10	13.2
814	Other textiles processing operatives	13.2	1	8.1	9.1	13.2	13.2	10	13.2
820	Chemical, gas and petroleum process plant operatives	11.2	1	8.1	9.1	11.2	11.2	10	11.2
821	Paper, wood and related process plant operatives	12.3	1	8.1	9.1	12.3	12.3	10	12.3
822	Cutting and slitting machine operatives (paper products etc)	12.3	1	8.1	9.1	12.3	12.3	10	12.3
823	Glass and ceramics furnace operatives, kilnsetters	12.3	1	8.1	9.1	12.3	12.3	10	12.3
824	Rubber process operatives, moulding machine operatives, tyre builders	12.3	1	8.1	9.1	12.3	12.3	10	12.3
825	Plastics process operatives, moulders and extruders	12.4	1	8.1	9.1	12.4	12.4	10	12.4
826	Synthetic fibre makers	11.2	1	8.1	9.1	11.2	11.2	10	11.2
829	Other chemicals, paper, plastics and related process operatives n.e.c.	12.3	1	8.1	9.1	12.3	12.3	10	12.3
830	Furnace operatives (metal)	12.3	1	8.1	9.1	12.3	12.3	10	12.3
831	Metal drawers	12.3	1	8.1	9.1	12.3	12.3	10	12.3
832	Rollers	12.3	1	8.1	9.1	12.3	12.3	10	12.3
833	Annealers, hardeners, temperers (metal)	12.3	1	8.1	9.1	12.3	12.3	10	12.3
834	Electroplaters, galvanisers, colour coaters	12.3	1	8.1	9.1	12.3	12.3	10	12.3

Please note: This derivation table has no empty cells. See key at end of table.

Table 14 - *continued*

Standard Occupational Classification 1990 unit group	Simplified NS-SEC	Employment status/size of organisation						
		1 Employers - large organisations	2 Employers - small organisations	3 Self-employed - no employees	4 Managers - large organisations	5 Managers - small organisations	6 Supervisors	7 Other employees
839 Other metal making and treating process operatives n.e.c.	12.3	1	8.1	9.1	12.3	12.3	10	12.3
840 Machine tool operatives (including CNC machine tool operatives)	12.4	1	8.1	9.1	12.4	12.4	10	12.4
841 Press stamping and automatic machine operatives	12.4	1	8.1	9.1	12.4	12.4	10	12.4
842 Metal polishers	12.4	1	8.1	9.1	12.4	12.4	10	12.4
843 Metal dressing operatives	12.4	1	8.1	9.1	12.4	12.4	10	12.4
844 Shot blasters	12.4	1	8.1	9.1	12.4	12.4	10	12.4
850 Assemblers/lineworkers (electrical/electronic goods)	12.4	1	8.1	9.1	12.4	12.4	10	12.4
851 Assemblers/lineworkers (vehicles and other metal goods)	12.4	1	8.1	9.1	12.4	12.4	10	12.4
859 Other assemblers/lineworkers n.e.c.	13.2	1	8.1	9.1	13.2	13.2	10	13.2
860 Inspectors, viewers and testers (metal and electrical goods)	11.2	1	8.1	9.1	11.2	11.2	10	11.2
861 Inspectors, viewers, testers and examiners (other manufactured goods)	11.2	1	8.1	9.1	11.2	11.2	10	11.2
862 Packers, bottlers, canners, fillers	13.2	1	8.1	9.1	13.2	13.2	10	13.2
863 Weighers, graders, sorters	13.2	1	8.1	9.1	13.2	13.2	10	13.2
864 Routine laboratory testers	7.3	1	8.1	9.1	7.3	7.3	6	7.3
869 Other routine process operatives n.e.c.	11.2	1	8.1	9.1	11.2	11.2	10	11.2
870 Bus inspectors	10	1	8.1	9.1	11.2	11.2	10	11.2
871 Road transport depot inspectors and related occupations	10	1	8.1	9.1	11.2	11.2	10	11.2
872 Drivers of road goods vehicles	13.3	1	8.1	9.1	13.3	13.3	10	13.3
873 Bus and coach drivers	13.3	1	8.1	9.1	13.3	13.3	10	13.3
874 Taxi, cab drivers and chauffeurs	9.1	1	8.1	9.1	13.3	13.3	10	13.3
875 Bus conductors	13.3	1	8.1	9.1	13.3	13.3	10	13.3
880 Seafarers (merchant navy); barge, lighter and boat operatives	12.4	1	8.1	9.1	12.4	12.4	10	12.4
881 Rail transport inspectors, supervisors and guards	11.2	1	8.1	9.1	11.2	11.2	10	11.2
882 Rail engine drivers and assistants	11.2	11.2	11.2	11.2	11.2	11.2	10	11.2
883 Rail signal operatives and crossing keepers	11.2	1	8.1	9.1	11.2	11.2	10	11.2
884 Shunters and points operatives	11.2	1	8.1	9.1	11.2	11.2	10	11.2
885 Mechanical plant drivers and operatives (earth moving and civil engineering)	13.3	1	8.1	9.1	13.3	13.3	10	13.3
886 Crane drivers	12.3	1	8.1	9.1	12.3	12.3	10	12.3
887 Fork lift and mechanical truck drivers	12.3	1	8.1	9.1	12.3	12.3	10	12.3
889 Other transport and machinery operatives n.e.c.	13.4	1	8.1	9.1	13.4	13.4	10	13.4
890 Washers, screeners and crushers in mines and quarries	11.2	1	8.1	9.1	11.2	11.2	10	11.2
891 Printing machine minders and assistants	12.3	1	8.1	9.1	12.3	12.3	10	12.3
892 Water and sewerage plant attendants	11.2	1	8.1	9.1	11.2	11.2	10	11.2
893 Electrical, energy, boiler and related plant operatives and attendants	12.4	1	8.1	9.1	12.4	12.4	10	12.4
894 Oilers, greasers, lubricators	12.4	1	8.1	9.1	12.4	12.4	10	12.4
895 Mains and service pipe layers, pipe jointers	13.4	1	8.1	9.1	13.4	13.4	10	13.4
896 Construction and related operatives	10	1	8.1	9.1	10	10	10	13.4
897 Woodworking machine operatives	12.3	1	8.1	9.1	12.3	12.3	10	12.3
898 Mine (excluding coal) and quarry workers	11.2	1	8.1	9.1	11.2	11.2	10	11.2
899 Other plant and machine operatives n.e.c.	12.4	1	8.1	9.1	10	10	10	12.4
900 Farm workers	12.5	1	8.2	9.2	12.5	12.5	6	12.5
901 Agricultural machinery drivers and operatives	12.5	1	8.2	9.2	12.5	12.5	10	12.5
902 All other occupations in farming and related	13.5	1	8.2	9.2	13.5	13.5	10	13.5
903 Fishing and related workers	9.1	1	8.1	9.1	13.5	13.5	10	13.5
904 Forestry workers	9.2	1	8.2	9.2	12.5	12.5	10	12.5
910 Coal mine labourers	13.3	1	8.1	9.1	13.3	13.3	10	13.3
911 Labourers in foundries	13.4	1	8.1	9.1	13.4	13.4	10	13.4
912 Labourers in engineering and allied trades	13.4	1	8.1	9.1	13.4	13.4	10	13.4
913 Mates to metal/electrical and related fitters	13.4	1	8.1	9.1	13.4	13.4	10	13.4

Please note: This derivation table has no empty cells. See key at end of table.

Table 14 - *continued*

Standard Occupational Classification 1990 unit group		Simplified NS-SEC	Employment status/size of organisation						
			1 Employers - large organisations	2 Employers - small organisations	3 Self-employed - no employees	4 Managers - large organisations	5 Managers - small organisations	6 Supervisors	7 Other employees
919	Other labourers in making and processing industries n.e.c.	13.4	1	8.1	9.1	13.4	13.4	10	13.4
920	Mates to woodworking trades workers	13.4	1	8.1	9.1	13.4	13.4	10	13.4
921	Mates to building trades workers	9.1	1	8.1	9.1	13.4	13.4	10	13.4
922	Rail construction and maintenance workers	11.2	1	8.1	9.1	11.2	11.2	10	11.2
923	Road construction and maintenance workers	10	1	8.1	9.1	12.4	12.4	10	12.4
924	Paviors, kerb layers	9.1	1	8.1	9.1	12.4	12.4	10	12.4
929	Other building and civil engineering labourers n.e.c.	13.4	1	8.1	9.1	13.4	13.4	10	13.4
930	Stevedores, dockers	13.4	1	8.1	9.1	13.4	13.4	10	13.4
931	Goods porters	13.4	1	8.1	9.1	12.4	12.4	10	13.4
932	Slingers	13.4	1	8.1	9.1	13.4	13.4	10	13.4
933	Refuse and salvage collectors	13.4	1	8.1	9.1	13.4	13.4	10	13.4
934	Driver's mates	13.4	1	8.1	9.1	13.4	13.4	10	13.4
940	Postal workers, mail sorters	12.2	1	8.1	9.1	12.2	12.2	10	12.2
941	Messengers, couriers	12.2	1	8.1	9.1	12.2	12.2	10	12.2
950	Hospital porters	12.2	1	8.1	9.1	12.2	12.2	10	12.2
951	Hotel porters	13.1	1	8.1	9.1	13.1	13.1	10	13.1
952	Kitchen porters, hands	12.2	1	8.1	9.1	12.2	12.2	10	12.2
953	Counterhands, catering assistants	12.2	1	8.1	9.1	12.2	12.2	10	12.2
954	Shelf fillers	12.1	1	8.1	9.1	12.1	12.1	10	12.1
955	Lift and car park attendants	13.4	1	8.1	9.1	13.4	13.4	10	13.4
956	Window cleaners	9.1	1	8.1	9.1	13.2	13.2	10	13.2
957	Road sweepers	13.4	1	8.1	9.1	13.4	13.4	10	13.4
958	Cleaners, domestics	13.4	1	8.1	9.1	13.4	13.4	10	13.4
959	Other occupations in sales and services n.e.c.	13.4	1	8.1	9.1	13.4	13.4	10	13.4
990	All other labourers and related workers	13.4	1	8.1	9.1	13.4	13.4	10	13.4
999	All others in miscellaneous occupations n.e.c.	13.1	1	8.1	9.1	13.1	13.1	10	13.1

Please note: This derivation table has no empty cells.

Cells filled by the developers in April 2001.
Cells filled by using the priority order rules (see Appendix A).

Table 15

NS-SEC based on SOC90 simplified and full derivation table: analytic classes

Standard Occupational Classification 1990 unit group	Simplified NS-SEC	Employment status/size of organisation						
		1 Employers - large organisations	2 Employers - small organisations	3 Self-employed - no employees	4 Managers - large organisations	5 Managers - small organisations	6 Supervisors	7 Other employees
100 General administrators; national government (Assistant Secretary/Grade 5 and above)	1.1	1.1	1.1	1.1	1.1	1.1	1.1	1.1
101 General managers; large companies and organisations	1.1	1.1	1.1	1.1	1.1	1.1	1.1	1.1
102 Local government officers (administrative and executive functions)	1.1	4	4	4	1.1	1.1	1.1	1.1
103 General administrators; national government (HEO to Senior Principal/Grade 6)	2	2	2	2	2	2	2	2
110 Production, works and maintenance managers	1.1	1.1	4	4	1.1	2	2	2
111 Managers in building and contracting	2	1.1	4	4	2	2	2	2
112 Clerks of works	2	1.1	4	4	2	2	2	2
113 Managers in mining and energy industries	1.1	1.1	4	4	1.1	2	2	2
120 Treasurers and company financial managers	1.1	1.2	1.2	1.2	1.1	1.1	1.1	1.1
121 Marketing and sales managers	1.1	1.1	4	2	1.1	2	2	2
122 Purchasing managers	1.1	1.1	4	4	1.1	2	2	2
123 Advertising and public relations managers	1.1	1.1	4	2	1.1	2	2	2
124 Personnel, training and industrial relations managers	1.1	1.1	4	4	1.1	2	2	2
125 Organisation and methods and work study managers	1.1	1.1	4	4	1.1	2	2	2
126 Computer systems and data processing managers	1.1	1.1	4	4	1.1	2	2	2
127 Company secretaries	3	1.1	4	4	3	3	2	3
130 Credit controllers	3	1.1	4	4	3	3	2	3
131 Bank, Building Society and Post Office managers (except self-employed)	2	1.1	4	4	2	2	2	2
132 Civil Service executive officers	2	2	2	2	2	2	2	2
139 Other financial institution and office managers n.e.c.	2	1.1	4	4	2	2	2	2
140 Transport managers	2	1.1	4	4	2	2	2	2
141 Stores controllers	6	1.1	4	4	6	2	2	2
142 Managers in warehousing and other materials handling	2	1.1	4	4	2	2	2	2
150 Officers in UK armed forces	1.1	1.1	1.1	1.1	1.1	1.1	1.1	1.1
151 Officers in foreign and Commonwealth armed forces	1.1	1.1	1.1	1.1	1.1	1.1	1.1	1.1
152 Police officers (inspector and above)	1.1	1.1	1.1	1.1	1.1	1.1	1.1	1.1
153 Fire service officers (station officer and above)	1.1	1.1	1.1	1.1	1.1	1.1	1.1	1.1
154 Prison officers (principal officer and above)	1.1	1.1	1.1	1.1	1.1	1.1	1.1	1.1
155 Customs and excise, immigration service officers (customs: chief preventive officer and above; excise: surveyor and above)	1.1	1.1	1.1	1.1	1.1	1.1	1.1	1.1
160 Farm owners and managers, horticulturists	4	1.1	4	4	2	2	2	2
169 Other managers in farming, horticulture, forestry and fishing n.e.c.	4	1.1	4	4	5	2	2	2
170 Property and estate managers	2	1.1	4	4	1.1	2	2	2
171 Garage managers and proprietors	4	1.1	4	4	2	2	2	2
172 Hairdressers' and barbers' managers and proprietors	4	1.1	4	4	2	2	2	2
173 Hotel and accommodation managers	4	1.1	4	4	2	2	2	2
174 Restaurant and catering managers	2	1.1	4	4	2	2	2	2
175 Publicans, innkeepers and club stewards	2	1.1	4	4	2	2	2	2

Please note: This derivation table has no empty cells. See key at the end of table.

Table 15 - *continued*

Standard Occupational Classification 1990 unit group	Simplified NS-SEC	Employment status/size of organisation						
		1 Employers - large organisations	2 Employers - small organisations	3 Self-employed - no employees	4 Managers - large organisations	5 Managers - small organisations	6 Supervisors	7 Other employees
176 Entertainment and sports managers	2	1.1	4	4	2	2	2	2
177 Travel agency managers	2	1.1	4	4	2	2	2	2
178 Managers and proprietors of butchers and fishmongers	4	1.1	4	4	2	2	2	2
179 Managers and proprietors in service industries n.e.c.	2	1.1	4	4	2	2	2	2
190 Officials of trade associations, trade unions, professional bodies and charities	2	1.1	4	4	1.1	2	2	2
191 Registrars and administrators of educational establishments	1.2	1.2	1.2	1.2	1.2	1.2	1.2	1.2
199 Other managers and administrators n.e.c.	2	1.1	4	4	2	2	2	2
200 Chemists	1.2	1.2	1.2	1.2	1.1	2	1.2	1.2
201 Biological scientists and biochemists	1.2	1.2	1.2	1.2	1.1	2	1.2	1.2
202 Physicists, geologists and meteorologists	1.2	1.2	1.2	1.2	1.1	2	1.2	1.2
209 Other natural scientists n.e.c.	1.2	1.2	1.2	1.2	1.2	1.2	1.2	1.2
210 Civil, structural, municipal, mining and quarrying engineers	1.2	1.2	1.2	1.2	1.2	1.2	1.2	1.2
211 Mechanical engineers	1.2	1.2	1.2	1.2	1.2	1.2	1.2	1.2
212 Electrical engineers	1.2	1.2	1.2	1.2	1.2	1.2	1.2	1.2
213 Electronic engineers	1.2	1.2	1.2	1.2	1.2	1.2	1.2	1.2
214 Software engineers	1.2	1.2	1.2	1.2	1.2	1.2	1.2	1.2
215 Chemical engineers	1.2	1.2	1.2	1.2	1.2	1.2	1.2	1.2
216 Design and development engineers	1.2	1.2	1.2	1.2	1.2	1.2	1.2	1.2
217 Process and production engineers	2	1.1	2	2	2	2	2	2
218 Planning and quality control engineers	2	1.1	2	2	2	2	2	2
219 Other engineers and technologists n.e.c.	1.2	1.2	1.2	1.2	1.2	1.2	1.2	1.2
220 Medical practitioners	1.2	1.2	1.2	1.2	1.2	1.2	1.2	1.2
221 Pharmacists/pharmacologists	1.2	1.2	1.2	1.2	1.1	2	1.2	1.2
222 Ophthalmic opticians	2	1.1	2	2	2	2	2	2
223 Dental practitioners	1.2	1.2	1.2	1.2	1.2	1.2	1.2	1.2
224 Veterinarians	1.2	1.2	1.2	1.2	1.2	1.2	1.2	1.2
230 University and polytechnic teaching professionals	1.2	1.2	1.2	1.2	1.2	1.2	1.2	1.2
231 Higher and further education teaching professionals	2	1.1	2	2	2	2	2	2
232 Education officers, school inspectors	1.2	1.2	1.2	1.2	1.2	1.2	1.2	1.2
233 Secondary (and middle school deemed secondary) education teaching professionals	2	1.1	2	2	2	2	2	2
234 Primary (and middle school deemed primary) and nursery education teaching professionals	2	1.1	2	2	2	2	2	2
235 Special education teaching professionals	2	1.1	2	2	2	2	2	2
239 Other teaching professionals n.e.c.	4	1.1	4	4	3	3	2	3
240 Judges and officers of the Court	1.2	1.2	1.2	1.2	1.2	1.2	1.2	1.2
241 Barristers and advocates	1.2	1.2	1.2	1.2	1.2	1.2	1.2	1.2
242 Solicitors	1.2	1.2	1.2	1.2	1.2	1.2	1.2	1.2
250 Chartered and certified accountants	1.2	1.2	1.2	1.2	1.2	1.2	1.2	1.2
251 Management accountants	1.2	1.2	1.2	1.2	1.2	1.2	1.2	1.2
252 Actuaries, economists and statisticians	1.2	1.2	1.2	1.2	1.2	1.2	1.2	1.2
253 Management consultants, business analysts	1.2	1.2	1.2	1.2	1.2	1.2	1.2	1.2
260 Architects	1.2	1.2	1.2	1.2	1.2	1.2	1.2	1.2
261 Town planners	1.2	1.2	1.2	1.2	1.2	1.2	1.2	1.2
262 Building, land, mining and 'general practice' surveyors	1.2	1.2	1.2	1.2	1.2	1.2	1.2	1.2
270 Librarians	2	2	2	2	2	2	2	2
271 Archivists and curators	2	2	2	2	2	2	2	2
290 Psychologists	1.2	1.2	1.2	1.2	1.2	1.2	1.2	1.2
291 Other social and behavioural scientists	1.2	1.2	1.2	1.2	1.2	1.2	1.2	1.2
292 Clergy	1.2	1.2	1.2	1.2	1.2	1.2	1.2	1.2
293 Social workers, probation officers	2	2	2	2	2	2	2	2
300 Laboratory technicians	2	1.1	2	2	2	2	2	2
301 Engineering technicians	2	1.1	2	2	2	2	2	2
302 Electrical/electronic technicians	3	1.1	4	4	3	3	2	3
303 Architectural and town planning technicians	2	1.1	2	2	2	2	2	2

Please note: This derivation table has no empty cells. See key at the end of table.

Table 15 - *continued*

Standard Occupational Classification 990 unit group	Simplified NS-SEC	Employment status/size of organisation						
		1 Employers - large organisations	2 Employers - small organisations	3 Self-employed - no employees	4 Managers - large organisations	5 Managers - small organisations	6 Supervisors	7 Other employees
304 Building and civil engineering technicians	2	1.1	2	2	2	2	2	2
309 Other scientific technicians n.e.c.	2	1.1	2	2	2	2	2	2
310 Draughtspersons	3	1.1	4	4	3	3	2	3
311 Building inspectors	2	2	2	2	2	2	2	2
312 Quantity surveyors	2	1.1	2	2	2	2	2	2
313 Marine, insurance and other surveyors	2	1.2	1.2	1.2	2	2	1.2	2
320 Computer analyst/programmers	1.2	1.2	1.2	1.2	1.2	1.2	1.2	1.2
330 Air traffic planners and controllers	2	2	2	2	2	2	2	2
331 Aircraft flight deck officers	1.2	1.2	1.2	1.2	1.2	1.2	1.2	1.2
332 Ship and hovercraft officers	2	1.1	2	2	2	2	2	2
340 Nurses	2	1.1	4	2	2	2	2	2
341 Midwives	2	1.1	2	2	2	2	2	2
342 Medical radiographers	2	1.1	2	2	2	2	2	2
343 Physiotherapists	2	1.1	2	2	2	2	2	2
344 Chiropodists	2	1.1	2	2	2	2	2	2
345 Dispensing opticians	3	1.1	4	4	3	3	2	3
346 Medical technicians, dental auxiliaries	6	1.1	4	4	3	3	5	6
347 Occupational and speech therapists, psychotherapists, therapists n.e.c.	2	1.1	2	2	2	2	2	2
348 Environmental health officers	1.2	1.2	1.2	1.2	1.2	1.2	1.2	1.2
349 Other health associate professionals n.e.c.	6	1.1	4	4	6	6	5	6
350 Legal service and related occupations	3	1.1	1.2	4	3	3	2	3
360 Estimators, valuers	2	1.1	2	2	2	2	2	2
361 Underwriters, claims assessors brokers, investment analysts	2	1.1	2	2	1.2	2	2	2
362 Taxation experts	1.2	1.2	1.2	1.2	1.2	1.2	1.2	1.2
363 Personnel and industrial relations officers	2	1.1	2	2	2	2	2	2
364 Organisation and methods and work study officers	1.2	1.2	1.2	1.2	1.2	1.2	1.2	1.2
370 Matrons, houseparents	6	1.1	4	4	5	5	5	6
371 Welfare, community and youth workers	2	1.1	2	2	2	2	2	2
380 Authors, writers, journalists	2	1.1	2	2	2	2	2	2
381 Artists, commercial artists, graphic designers	4	1.1	4	4	3	3	2	3
382 Industrial designers	4	1.1	4	4	2	2	2	3
383 Clothing designers	3	1.1	4	4	2	2	2	3
384 Actors, entertainers, stage managers, producers and directors	2	1.1	2	2	2	2	2	2
385 Musicians	2	1.1	2	2	2	2	2	2
386 Photographers, camera, sound and video equipment operators	3	1.1	4	4	3	3	2	3
387 Professional athletes, sports officials	2	1.1	2	2	2	2	2	2
390 Information officers	2	1.1	2	2	2	2	2	2
391 Vocational and industrial trainers	2	1.1	2	2	2	2	2	2
392 Careers advisers and vocational guidance specialists	2	1.1	2	2	2	2	2	2
393 Driving instructors (excluding HGV)	4	1.1	4	4	6	6	5	6
394 Inspectors of factories, utilities and trading standards	2	2	2	2	2	2	2	2
395 Other statutory and similar inspectors n.e.c.	2	2	2	2	2	2	2	2
396 Occupational hygienists and safety officers (health and safety)	2	1.1	2	2	2	2	2	2
399 Other associate professional and technical occupations n.e.c.	2	1.1	2	2	1.1	2	2	2
400 Civil Service administrative officers and assistants	3	3	3	3	3	3	2	3
401 Local government clerical officers and assistants	3	3	3	3	3	3	2	3
410 Accounts and wages clerks, book-keepers, other financial clerks	3	1.1	4	4	3	3	2	3
411 Counter clerks and cashiers	3	1.1	4	4	3	3	2	3
412 Debt, rent and other cash collectors	3	1.1	4	4	3	3	2	3
420 Filing, computer and other records clerks (including legal conveyancing)	3	1.1	4	4	3	3	2	3
421 Library assistants/clerks	3	1.1	4	4	3	3	2	3
430 Clerks (n.o.s.)	3	1.1	4	4	3	3	2	3
440 Stores, despatch and production control clerks	6	1.1	4	4	6	6	5	6

Please note: This derivation table has no empty cells. See key at the end of table.

Table 15 - *continued*

Standard Occupational Classification 1990 unit group		Simplified NS-SEC	Employment status/size of organisation						
			1 Employers - large organisations	2 Employers - small organisations	3 Self-employed - no employees	4 Managers - large organisations	5 Managers - small organisations	6 Supervisors	7 Other employees
441	Storekeepers and warehousemen/women	7	1.1	4	4	6	6	5	7
450	Medical secretaries	3	1.1	4	4	3	3	2	3
451	Legal secretaries	3	1.1	4	4	3	3	2	3
452	Typists and word processor operators	3	1.1	4	4	3	3	2	3
459	Other secretaries, personal assistants, typists, word processor operators n.e.c.	3	1.1	4	4	3	3	2	3
460	Receptionists	6	1.1	4	4	6	6	5	6
461	Receptionist/telephonists	6	1.1	4	4	6	6	5	6
462	Telephone operators	6	1.1	4	4	6	6	5	6
463	Radio and telegraph operators, other office communication system operators	5	1.1	4	4	5	5	5	5
490	Computer operators, data processing operators, other office machine operators	3	1.1	4	4	3	3	2	3
491	Tracers, drawing office assistants	3	1.1	4	4	3	3	2	3
500	Bricklayers, masons	4	1.1	4	4	7	7	5	7
501	Roofers, slaters, tilers, sheeters, cladders	4	1.1	4	4	7	7	5	7
502	Plasterers	4	1.1	4	4	7	7	5	7
503	Glaziers	7	1.1	4	4	7	7	5	7
504	Builders, building contractors	4	1.1	4	4	6	6	5	6
505	Scaffolders, stagers, steeplejacks, riggers	6	1.1	4	4	6	6	5	6
506	Floorers, floor coverers, carpet fitters and planners, floor and wall tilers	4	1.1	4	4	7	7	5	7
507	Painters and decorators	4	1.1	4	4	7	7	5	7
509	Other construction trades n.e.c.	4	1.1	4	4	6	6	5	6
510	Centre, capstan, turret and other lathe setters and setter-operators	6	1.1	4	4	6	6	5	6
511	Boring and drilling machine setters and setter-operators	6	1.1	4	4	6	6	5	6
512	Grinding machine setters and setter-operators	6	1.1	4	4	6	6	5	6
513	Milling machine setters and setter-operators	6	1.1	4	4	6	6	5	6
514	Press setters and setter-operators	5	1.1	4	4	6	6	5	6
515	Tool makers, tool fitters and markers-out	5	1.1	4	4	5	5	5	5
516	Metal working production and maintenance fitters	5	1.1	4	4	5	5	5	5
517	Precision instrument makers and repairers	5	1.1	4	4	5	5	5	5
518	Goldsmiths, silversmiths, precious stone workers	5	1.1	4	4	5	5	5	5
519	Other machine tool setters and setter-operators n.e.c. (including CNC setter-operators)	6	1.1	4	4	6	6	5	6
520	Production fitters (electrical/electronic)	5	1.1	4	4	5	5	5	5
521	Electricians, electrical maintenance fitters	5	1.1	4	4	5	5	5	5
522	Electrical engineers (not professional)	5	1.1	4	4	5	5	5	5
523	Telephone fitters	3	1.1	4	4	3	3	2	3
524	Cable jointers, lines repairers	5	1.1	4	4	5	5	5	5
525	Radio, TV and video engineers	5	1.1	4	4	5	5	5	5
526	Computer engineers, installation and maintenance	3	1.1	4	4	3	3	2	3
529	Other electrical/electronic trades n.e.c.	3	1.1	4	4	3	3	2	3
530	Smiths and forge workers	7	1.1	4	4	7	7	5	7
531	Moulders, core makers, die casters	6	1.1	4	4	6	6	5	6
532	Plumbers, heating and ventilating engineers and related trades	5	1.1	4	4	5	5	5	5
533	Sheet metal workers	6	1.1	4	4	6	6	5	6
534	Metal plate workers, shipwrights, riveters	7	1.1	4	4	7	7	5	7
535	Steel erectors	6	1.1	4	4	6	6	5	6
536	Barbenders, steel fixers	4	1.1	4	4	6	6	5	6
537	Welding trades	7	1.1	4	4	7	7	5	7
540	Motor mechanics, auto engineers (including road patrol engineers)	5	1.1	4	4	5	5	5	5
541	Coach and vehicle body builders	5	1.1	4	4	5	5	5	5

Please note: This derivation table has no empty cells. See key at the end of table.

Table 15 - *continued*

Standard Occupational Classification 1990 unit group	Simplified NS-SEC	Employment status/size of organisation						
		1 Employers - large organisations	2 Employers - small organisations	3 Self-employed - no employees	4 Managers - large organisations	5 Managers - small organisations	6 Supervisors	7 Other employees
542　Vehicle body repairers, panel beaters	5	1.1	4	4	5	5	5	5
543　Auto electricians	5	1.1	4	4	5	5	5	5
544　Tyre and exhaust fitters	6	1.1	4	4	6	6	5	6
550　Weavers	7	1.1	4	4	7	7	5	7
551　Knitters	7	1.1	4	4	7	7	5	7
552　Warp preparers, bleachers, dyers and finishers	7	1.1	4	4	7	7	5	7
553　Sewing machinists, menders, darners and embroiderers	7	1.1	4	4	7	7	5	7
554　Coach trimmers, upholsterers and mattress makers	7	1.1	4	4	7	7	5	7
555　Shoe repairers, leather cutters and sewers, footwear lasters, makers and finishers, other leather making and repairing	7	1.1	4	4	7	7	5	7
556　Tailors and dressmakers	4	1.1	4	4	6	6	5	6
557　Clothing cutters, milliners, furriers	6	1.1	4	4	6	6	5	6
559　Other textiles, garments and related trades n.e.c.	7	1.1	4	4	7	7	5	7
560　Originators, compositors and print preparers	5	1.1	4	4	5	5	5	5
561　Printers	5	1.1	4	4	5	5	5	5
562　Bookbinders and print finishers	7	1.1	4	4	7	7	5	7
563　Screen printers	5	1.1	4	4	5	5	5	5
569　Other printing and related trades n.e.c.	5	1.1	4	4	5	5	5	5
570　Carpenters and joiners	4	1.1	4	4	7	7	5	7
571　Cabinet makers	7	1.1	4	4	7	7	5	7
572　Case and box makers	6	1.1	4	4	6	6	5	6
573　Pattern makers (moulds)	5	1.1	4	4	5	5	5	5
579　Other woodworking trades n.e.c.	4	1.1	4	4	7	7	5	7
580　Bakers, flour confectioners	5	1.1	4	4	5	5	5	5
581　Butchers, meat cutters	7	1.1	4	4	7	7	5	7
582　Fishmongers, poultry dressers	7	1.1	4	4	7	7	5	7
590　Glass product and ceramics makers	7	1.1	4	4	7	7	5	7
591　Glass product and ceramics finishers and decorators	7	1.1	4	4	7	7	5	7
592　Dental technicians	3	1.1	4	4	3	3	2	3
593　Musical instrument makers, piano tuners	4	1.1	4	4	5	5	5	5
594　Gardeners, groundsmen/groundswomen	5	1.1	4	4	5	5	5	5
595　Horticultural trades	6	1.1	4	4	6	6	5	6
596　Coach painters, other spray painters	6	1.1	4	4	6	6	5	6
597　Face trained coalmining workers, shotfirers and deputies	7	1.1	4	4	7	7	5	7
598　Office machinery mechanics	3	1.1	4	4	3	3	2	3
599　Other craft and related occupations n.e.c.	5	1.1	4	4	5	5	5	5
600　NCOs and other ranks, UK armed forces	3	3	3	3	3	3	2	3
601　NCOs and other ranks, foreign and Commonwealth armed forces	3	3	3	3	3	3	2	3
610　Police officers (sergeant and below)	3	3	3	3	3	3	2	3
611　Fire service officers (leading fire officer and below)	3	3	3	3	3	3	2	3
612　Prison service officers (below principal officer)	3	3	3	3	3	3	2	3
613　Customs and excise officers, immigration officers (customs: below chief preventive officer; excise: below surveyor)	2	2	2	2	2	2	2	2
614　Traffic wardens	6	6	6	6	6	6	5	6
615　Security guards and related occupations	6	1.1	4	4	2	2	5	6
619　Other security and protective service occupations n.e.c.	7	1.1	4	4	7	7	5	7
620　Chefs, cooks	6	1.1	4	4	5	5	5	6
621　Waiters, waitresses	7	1.1	4	4	7	7	5	7
622　Bar staff	7	1.1	4	4	7	7	5	7
630　Travel and flight attendants	7	1.1	4	4	7	7	2	7
631　Railway station staff	5	1.1	4	4	5	5	5	5
640　Assistant nurses, nursing auxiliaries	3	1.1	4	4	3	3	2	3
641　Hospital ward assistants	3	1.1	4	4	3	3	2	3
642　Ambulance staff	3	3	3	3	3	3	2	3

Please note: This derivation table has no empty cells. See key at the end of table.

Table 15 - *continued*

Standard Occupational Classification 1990 unit group		Simplified NS-SEC	Employment status/size of organisation						
			1 Employers - large organisations	2 Employers - small organisations	3 Self-employed - no employees	4 Managers - large organisations	5 Managers - small organisations	6 Supervisors	7 Other employees
643	Dental nurses	6	1.1	4	4	6	6	5	6
644	Care assistants and attendants	6	1.1	4	4	6	6	5	6
650	Nursery nurses	3	1.1	4	4	3	3	2	3
651	Playgroup leaders	6	1.1	4	4	6	6	5	6
652	Educational assistants	6	1.1	4	4	6	6	5	6
659	Other childcare and related occupations n.e.c.	7	1.1	4	4	7	7	5	7
660	Hairdressers, barbers	7	1.1	4	4	7	7	5	7
661	Beauticians and related occupations	4	1.1	4	4	6	6	5	6
670	Domestic housekeepers and related occupations	6	1.1	4	4	6	6	5	6
671	Housekeepers (non-domestic)	5	1.1	4	4	6	6	5	6
672	Caretakers	6	1.1	4	4	6	6	5	6
673	Launderers, dry cleaners, pressers	7	1.1	4	4	7	7	5	7
690	Undertakers	6	1.1	4	4	6	6	5	6
691	Bookmakers	2	1.1	4	4	2	2	5	6
699	Other personal and protective service occupations n.e.c.	6	1.1	4	4	6	6	5	6
700	Buyers (retail trade)	2	1.1	2	2	2	2	2	2
701	Buyers and purchasing officers (not retail)	2	1.1	2	2	2	2	2	2
702	Importers and exporters	2	1.1	2	2	2	2	2	2
703	Air, commodity and ship brokers	1.2	1.2	1.2	1.2	1.2	1.2	1.2	1.2
710	Technical and wholesale sales representatives	2	1.1	2	2	1.1	2	2	2
719	Other sales representatives n.e.c.	3	1.1	2	2	2	2	2	3
720	Sales assistants	6	1.1	4	4	6	6	5	6
721	Retail cash desk and check-out operators	6	1.1	4	4	6	6	5	6
722	Petrol pump forecourt attendants	6	1.1	4	4	6	6	5	6
730	Collector salespersons and credit agents	4	1.1	4	4	6	6	5	6
731	Roundsmen/women and van salespersons	7	1.1	4	4	7	7	5	7
732	Market and street traders and assistants	4	1.1	4	4	7	7	5	7
733	Scrap dealers, scrap metal merchants	4	1.1	4	4	2	2	2	2
790	Merchandisers	3	1.1	4	4	3	3	2	3
791	Window dressers, floral arrangers	7	1.1	4	4	7	7	5	7
792	Telephone salespersons	6	1.1	4	4	6	6	5	6
800	Bakery and confectionery process operatives	6	1.1	4	4	6	6	5	6
801	Brewery and vinery process operatives	6	1.1	4	4	6	6	5	6
802	Tobacco process operatives	6	1.1	4	4	6	6	5	6
809	Other food, drink and tobacco process operatives n.e.c.	6	1.1	4	4	6	6	5	6
810	Tannery production operatives	5	1.1	4	4	5	5	5	5
811	Preparatory fibre processors	7	1.1	4	4	7	7	5	7
812	Spinners, doublers, twisters	7	1.1	4	4	7	7	5	7
813	Winders, reelers	7	1.1	4	4	7	7	5	7
814	Other textiles processing operatives	7	1.1	4	4	7	7	5	7
820	Chemical, gas and petroleum process plant operatives	5	1.1	4	4	5	5	5	5
821	Paper, wood and related process plant operatives	6	1.1	4	4	6	6	5	6
822	Cutting and slitting machine operatives (paper products etc)	6	1.1	4	4	6	6	5	6
823	Glass and ceramics furnace operatives, kilnsetters	6	1.1	4	4	6	6	5	6
824	Rubber process operatives, moulding machine operatives, tyre builders	6	1.1	4	4	6	6	5	6
825	Plastics process operatives, moulders and extruders	6	1.1	4	4	6	6	5	6
826	Synthetic fibre makers	5	1.1	4	4	5	5	5	5
829	Other chemicals, paper, plastics and related process operatives n.e.c.	6	1.1	4	4	6	6	5	6
830	Furnace operatives (metal)	6	1.1	4	4	6	6	5	6
831	Metal drawers	6	1.1	4	4	6	6	5	6
832	Rollers	6	1.1	4	4	6	6	5	6
833	Annealers, hardeners, temperers (metal)	6	1.1	4	4	6	6	5	6
834	Electroplaters, galvanisers, colour coaters	6	1.1	4	4	6	6	5	6

Please note: This derivation table has no empty cells. See key at the end of table.

Table 15 - *continued*

Standard Occupational Classification 1990 unit group		Simplified NS-SEC	Employment status/size of organisation						
			1 Employers - large organisations	2 Employers - small organisations	3 Self-employed - no employees	4 Managers - large organisations	5 Managers - small organisations	6 Supervisors	7 Other employees
839	Other metal making and treating process operatives n.e.c.	6	1.1	4	4	6	6	5	6
840	Machine tool operatives (including CNC machine tool operatives)	6	1.1	4	4	6	6	5	6
841	Press stamping and automatic machine operatives	6	1.1	4	4	6	6	5	6
842	Metal polishers	6	1.1	4	4	6	6	5	6
843	Metal dressing operatives	6	1.1	4	4	6	6	5	6
844	Shot blasters	6	1.1	4	4	6	6	5	6
850	Assemblers/lineworkers (electrical/ electronic goods)	6	1.1	4	4	6	6	5	6
851	Assemblers/lineworkers (vehicles and other metal goods)	6	1.1	4	4	6	6	5	6
859	Other assemblers/lineworkers n.e.c.	7	1.1	4	4	7	7	5	7
860	Inspectors, viewers and testers (metal and electrical goods)	5	1.1	4	4	5	5	5	5
861	Inspectors, viewers, testers and examiners (other manufactured goods)	5	1.1	4	4	5	5	5	5
862	Packers, bottlers, canners, fillers	7	1.1	4	4	7	7	5	7
863	Weighers, graders, sorters	7	1.1	4	4	7	7	5	7
864	Routine laboratory testers	3	1.1	4	4	3	3	2	3
869	Other routine process operatives n.e.c.	5	1.1	4	4	5	5	5	5
870	Bus inspectors	5	1.1	4	4	5	5	5	5
871	Road transport depot inspectors and related occupations	5	1.1	4	4	5	5	5	5
872	Drivers of road goods vehicles	7	1.1	4	4	7	7	5	7
873	Bus and coach drivers	7	1.1	4	4	7	7	5	7
874	Taxi, cab drivers and chauffeurs	4	1.1	4	4	7	7	5	7
875	Bus conductors	7	1.1	4	4	7	7	5	7
880	Seafarers (merchant navy); barge, lighter and boat operatives	6	1.1	4	4	6	6	5	6
881	Rail transport inspectors, supervisors and guards	5	1.1	4	4	5	5	5	5
882	Rail engine drivers and assistants	5	5	5	5	5	5	5	5
883	Rail signal operatives and crossing keepers	5	1.1	4	4	5	5	5	5
884	Shunters and points operatives	5	1.1	4	4	5	5	5	5
885	Mechanical plant drivers and operatives (earth moving and civil engineering)	7	1.1	4	4	7	7	5	7
886	Crane drivers	6	1.1	4	4	6	6	5	6
887	Fork lift and mechanical truck drivers	6	1.1	4	4	6	6	5	6
889	Other transport and machinery operatives n.e.c.	7	1.1	4	4	7	7	5	7
890	Washers, screeners and crushers in mines and quarries	5	1.1	4	4	5	5	5	5
891	Printing machine minders and assistants	6	1.1	4	4	6	6	5	6
892	Water and sewerage plant attendants	5	1.1	4	4	5	5	5	5
893	Electrical, energy, boiler and related plant operatives and attendants	6	1.1	4	4	6	6	5	6
894	Oilers, greasers, lubricators	6	1.1	4	4	6	6	5	6
895	Mains and service pipe layers, pipe jointers	7	1.1	4	4	7	7	5	7
896	Construction and related operatives	5	1.1	4	4	5	5	5	7
897	Woodworking machine operatives	6	1.1	4	4	6	6	5	6
898	Mine (excluding coal) and quarry workers	5	1.1	4	4	5	5	5	5
899	Other plant and machine operatives n.e.c.	6	1.1	4	4	5	5	5	6
900	Farm workers	6	1.1	4	4	6	6	2	6
901	Agricultural machinery drivers and operatives	6	1.1	4	4	6	6	5	6
902	All other occupations in farming and related	7	1.1	4	4	7	7	5	7
903	Fishing and related workers	4	1.1	4	4	7	7	5	7
904	Forestry workers	4	1.1	4	4	6	6	5	6
910	Coal mine labourers	7	1.1	4	4	7	7	5	7
911	Labourers in foundries	7	1.1	4	4	7	7	5	7
912	Labourers in engineering and allied trades	7	1.1	4	4	7	7	5	7
913	Mates to metal/electrical and related fitters	7	1.1	4	4	7	7	5	7

Please note: This derivation table has no empty cells. See key at the end of table.

Table 15 - *continued*

Standard Occupational Classification 1990 unit group		Simplified NS-SEC	Employment status/size of organisation						
			1 Employers - large organisations	2 Employers - small organisations	3 Self-employed - no employees	4 Managers - large organisations	5 Managers - small organisations	6 Supervisors	7 Other employees
919	Other labourers in making and processing industries n.e.c.	7	1.1	4	4	7	7	5	7
920	Mates to woodworking trades workers	7	1.1	4	4	7	7	5	7
921	Mates to building trades workers	4	1.1	4	4	7	7	5	7
922	Rail construction and maintenance workers	5	1.1	4	4	5	5	5	5
923	Road construction and maintenance workers	5	1.1	4	4	6	6	5	6
924	Paviors, kerb layers	4	1.1	4	4	6	6	5	6
929	Other building and civil engineering labourers n.e.c.	7	1.1	4	4	7	7	5	7
930	Stevedores, dockers	7	1.1	4	4	7	7	5	7
931	Goods porters	7	1.1	4	4	6	6	5	7
932	Slingers	7	1.1	4	4	7	7	5	7
933	Refuse and salvage collectors	7	1.1	4	4	7	7	5	7
934	Driver's mates	7	1.1	4	4	7	7	5	7
940	Postal workers, mail sorters	6	1.1	4	4	6	6	5	6
941	Messengers, couriers	6	1.1	4	4	6	6	5	6
950	Hospital porters	6	1.1	4	4	6	6	5	6
951	Hotel porters	7	1.1	4	4	7	7	5	7
952	Kitchen porters, hands	6	1.1	4	4	6	6	5	6
953	Counterhands, catering assistants	6	1.1	4	4	6	6	5	6
954	Shelf fillers	6	1.1	4	4	6	6	5	6
955	Lift and car park attendants	7	1.1	4	4	7	7	5	7
956	Window cleaners	4	1.1	4	4	7	7	5	7
957	Road sweepers	7	1.1	4	4	7	7	5	7
958	Cleaners, domestics	7	1.1	4	4	7	7	5	7
959	Other occupations in sales and services n.e.c.	7	1.1	4	4	7	7	5	7
990	All other labourers and related workers	7	1.1	4	4	7	7	5	7
999	All others in miscellaneous occupations n.e.c.	7	1.1	4	4	7	7	5	7

Please note: This derivation table has no empty cells.

Cells filled by the developers in April 2001.
Cells filled by using the priority order rules (see Appendix A).

Table 16

NS-SEC based on SOC90 simplified and reduced derivation table: operational categories

Standard Occupational Classification 1990 unit group		Simplified NS-SEC	Employment status				
			1 Employers	2 Self-employed - no employees	3 Managers	4 Supervisors	5 Other employees
100	General administrators; national government (Assistant Secretary/Grade 5 and above)	2	2	22	2	2	
101	General managers; large companies and organisations	2	2	22	2	2	
102	Local government officers (administrative and executive functions)	2	9.1	9.1	2	2	2
103	General administrators; national government (HEO to Senior Principal/Grade 6)	4.1	4.1	4.1	4.1	4.1	4.1
110	Production, works and maintenance managers	2	8.1	9.1	2	6	2
111	Managers in building and contracting	5	8.1	9.1	5	5	5
112	Clerks of works	5	8.1	9.1	5	5	5
113	Managers in mining and energy industries	2	8.1	9.1	2	2	2
120	Treasurers and company financial managers	2	3.3	3.3	2	2	2
121	Marketing and sales managers	2	8.1	4.3	2	2	2
122	Purchasing managers	2	8.1	9.1	2	2	2
123	Advertising and public relations managers	2	8.1	4.3	2	2	2
124	Personnel, training and industrial relations managers	2	8.1	9.1	2	2	2
125	Organisation and methods and work study managers	2	8.1	9.1	2	2	2
126	Computer systems and data processing managers	2	8.1	9.1	2	2	2
127	Company secretaries	7.1	8.1	9.1	7.1	6	7.1
130	Credit controllers	7.1	8.1	9.1	7.1	6	7.1
131	Bank, Building Society and Post Office managers (except self-employed)	5	8.1	9.1	5	5	5
132	Civil Service executive officers	4.1	4.1	4.1	4.1	4.1	4.1
139	Other financial institution and office managers n.e.c.	5	8.1	9.1	5	5	5
140	Transport managers	5	8.1	9.1	5	5	5
141	Stores controllers	12.6	8.1	9.1	12.6	12.6	12.6
142	Managers in warehousing and other materials handling	5	8.1	9.1	5	5	5
150	Officers in UK armed forces	2	2	22	2	2	
151	Officers in foreign and Commonwealth armed forces	2	2	22	2	2	
152	Police officers (inspector and above)	2	2	22	2	2	
153	Fire service officers (station officer and above)	2	2	22	2	2	
154	Prison officers (principal officer and above)	2	2	22	2	2	
155	Customs and excise, immigration service officers (customs: chief preventive officer and above; excise: surveyor and above)	2	2	22	2	2	
160	Farm owners and managers, horticulturists	9.2	8.2	9.2	5	6	5
169	Other managers in farming, horticulture, forestry and fishing n.e.c.	9.2	8.2	9.2	11.1	11.1	11.1
170	Property and estate managers	5	8.1	9.1	5	5	5
171	Garage managers and proprietors	8.1	8.1	9.1	5	5	5
172	Hairdressers' and barbers' managers and proprietors	9.1	8.1	9.1	5	5	5
173	Hotel and accommodation managers	9.1	8.1	9.1	5	5	5
174	Restaurant and catering managers	5	8.1	9.1	5	5	5
175	Publicans, innkeepers and club stewards	5	8.1	9.1	5	5	5
176	Entertainment and sports managers	5	8.1	9.1	5	5	5
177	Travel agency managers	5	8.1	9.1	5	5	5
178	Managers and proprietors of butchers and fishmongers	8.1	8.1	9.1	5	5	5
179	Managers and proprietors in service industries n.e.c.	5	8.1	9.1	5	5	5
190	Officials of trade associations, trade unions, professional bodies and charities	4.1	8.1	9.1	5	4.1	4.1
191	Registrars and administrators of educational establishments	3.1	3.1	3.1	3.1	3.1	3.1
199	Other managers and administrators n.e.c.	5	8.1	9.1	5	5	5
200	Chemists	3.1	3.3	3.3	5	3.1	3.1
201	Biological scientists and biochemists	3.1	3.3	3.3	5	3.1	3.1
202	Physicists, geologists and meteorologists	3.1	3.3	3.3	5	3.1	3.1
209	Other natural scientists n.e.c.	3.1	3.3	3.3	3.1	3.1	3.1

Please note: This derivation table has no empty cells. See key at the end of table.

Table 16 - *continued*

Standard Occupational Classification 1990 unit group		Simplified NS-SEC	Employment status				
			1 Employers	2 Self-employed - no employees	3 Managers	4 Supervisors	5 Other employees
210	Civil, structural, municipal, mining and quarrying engineers	3.1	3.3	3.3	3.1	3.1	3.1
211	Mechanical engineers	3.1	3.3	3.3	3.1	3.1	3.1
212	Electrical engineers	3.1	3.3	3.3	3.1	3.1	3.1
213	Electronic engineers	3.1	3.3	3.3	3.1	3.1	3.1
214	Software engineers	3.1	3.3	3.3	3.1	3.1	3.1
215	Chemical engineers	3.1	3.3	3.3	3.1	3.1	3.1
216	Design and development engineers	3.1	3.3	3.3	3.1	3.1	3.1
217	Process and production engineers	4.1	4.3	4.3	4.1	4.1	4.1
218	Planning and quality control engineers	4.1	4.3	4.3	5	4.1	4.1
219	Other engineers and technologists n.e.c.	3.1	3.3	3.3	3.1	3.1	3.1
220	Medical practitioners	3.1	3.3	3.3	3.1	3.1	3.1
221	Pharmacists/pharmacologists	3.1	3.3	3.3	5	3.1	3.1
222	Ophthalmic opticians	4.1	4.3	4.3	4.1	4.1	4.1
223	Dental practitioners	3.3	3.3	3.3	3.1	3.1	3.1
224	Veterinarians	3.1	3.3	3.3	3.1	3.1	3.1
230	University and polytechnic teaching professionals	3.1	3.3	3.3	3.1	3.1	3.1
231	Higher and further education teaching professionals	4.1	4.3	4.3	4.1	4.1	4.1
232	Education officers, school inspectors	3.1	3.1	3.1	3.1	3.1	3.1
233	Secondary (and middle school deemed secondary) education teaching professionals	4.1	4.3	4.3	4.1	4.1	4.1
234	Primary (and middle school deemed primary) and nursery education teaching professionals	4.1	4.3	4.3	4.1	4.1	4.1
235	Special education teaching professionals	4.1	4.3	4.3	4.1	4.1	4.1
239	Other teaching professionals n.e.c.	9.1	8.1	9.1	7.3	6	7.3
240	Judges and officers of the Court	3.1	3.3	3.3	3.1	3.1	3.1
241	Barristers and advocates	3.3	3.3	3.3	3.1	3.1	3.1
242	Solicitors	3.1	3.3	3.3	3.1	3.1	3.1
250	Chartered and certified accountants	3.1	3.3	3.3	3.1	3.1	3.1
251	Management accountants	3.2	3.4	3.4	3.2	3.2	3.2
252	Actuaries, economists and statisticians	3.1	3.3	3.3	3.1	3.1	3.1
253	Management consultants, business analysts	3.2	3.4	3.4	3.2	3.2	3.2
260	Architects	3.1	3.3	3.3	3.1	3.1	3.1
261	Town planners	3.1	3.3	3.3	3.1	3.1	3.1
262	Building, land, mining and 'general practice' surveyors	3.1	3.3	3.3	3.1	3.1	3.1
270	Librarians	4.1	4.3	4.3	4.1	4.1	4.1
271	Archivists and curators	4.1	4.3	4.3	4.1	4.1	4.1
290	Psychologists	3.1	3.3	3.3	3.1	3.1	3.1
291	Other social and behavioural scientists	3.1	3.3	3.3	3.1	3.1	3.1
292	Clergy	3.1	3.3	3.3	3.1	3.1	3.1
293	Social workers, probation officers	4.1	4.3	4.3	4.1	4.1	4.1
300	Laboratory technicians	4.1	4.3	4.3	4.1	4.1	4.1
301	Engineering technicians	4.1	4.3	4.3	4.1	4.1	4.1
302	Electrical/electronic technicians	7.3	8.1	9.1	7.3	6	7.3
303	Architectural and town planning technicians	4.1	4.3	4.3	4.1	4.1	4.1
304	Building and civil engineering technicians	4.1	4.3	4.3	4.1	4.1	4.1
309	Other scientific technicians n.e.c.	4.1	4.3	4.3	4.1	4.1	4.1
310	Draughtspersons	7.3	8.1	9.1	7.3	6	7.3
311	Building inspectors	4.1	4.3	4.3	4.1	4.1	4.1
312	Quantity surveyors	4.1	4.3	4.3	4.1	4.1	4.1
313	Marine, insurance and other surveyors	4.1	3.3	3.3	4.1	3.1	4.1
320	Computer analyst/programmers	3.2	3.4	3.4	3.2	3.2	3.2
330	Air traffic planners and controllers	4.1	4.1	4.1	4.1	4.1	4.1
331	Aircraft flight deck officers	3.2	3.4	3.4	3.2	3.2	3.2
332	Ship and hovercraft officers	4.1	4.3	4.3	4.1	4.1	4.1
340	Nurses	4.1	8.1	4.3	4.1	4.1	4.1
341	Midwives	4.1	4.3	4.3	4.1	4.1	4.1
342	Medical radiographers	4.1	4.3	4.3	4.1	4.1	4.1
343	Physiotherapists	4.1	4.3	4.3	4.1	4.1	4.1
344	Chiropodists	4.1	4.3	4.3	4.1	4.1	4.1
345	Dispensing opticians	7.3	8.1	9.1	7.3	6	7.3
346	Medical technicians, dental auxiliaries	12.1	8.1	9.1	7.3	10	12.1
347	Occupational and speech therapists, psychotherapists, therapists n.e.c.	4.1	4.3	4.3	4.1	4.1	4.1
348	Environmental health officers	3.2	3.2	3.2	3.2	3.2	3.2
349	Other health associate professionals n.e.c.	12.2	8.1	9.1	12.2	10	12.2
350	Legal service and related occupations	7.1	3.3	9.1	7.1	6	7.1
360	Estimators, valuers	4.1	4.3	4.3	4.1	4.1	4.1
361	Underwriters, claims assessors, brokers, investment analysts	4.1	4.3	4.3	3.2	4.1	4.1

Please note: This derivation table has no empty cells. See key at the end of table.

Table 16 - *continued*

Standard Occupational Classification 1990 unit group		Simplified NS-SEC	Employment status				
			1 Employers	2 Self-employed - no employees	3 Managers	4 Supervisors	5 Other employees
362	Taxation experts	3.2	3.4	3.4	3.2	3.2	3.2
363	Personnel and industrial relations officers	4.1	4.3	4.3	4.1	4.1	4.1
364	Organisation and methods and work study officers	3.1	3.3	3.3	3.1	3.1	3.1
370	Matrons, houseparents	12.7	8.1	9.1	10	10	12.7
371	Welfare, community and youth workers	4.1	4.3	4.3	4.1	4.1	4.1
380	Authors, writers, journalists	4.1	4.3	4.3	4.1	4.1	4.1
381	Artists, commercial artists, graphic designers	9.1	8.1	9.1	7.3	6	7.3
382	Industrial designers	9.1	8.1	9.1	6	6	7.3
383	Clothing designers	7.3	8.1	9.1	6	6	7.3
384	Actors, entertainers, stage managers, producers and directors	4.3	4.3	4.3	4.1	4.1	4.1
385	Musicians	4.3	4.3	4.3	4.1	4.1	4.1
386	Photographers, camera, sound and video equipment operators	7.3	8.1	9.1	7.3	6	7.3
387	Professional athletes, sports officials	4.2	4.4	4.4	4.2	4.2	4.2
390	Information officers	4.1	4.3	4.3	4.1	4.1	4.1
391	Vocational and industrial trainers	4.1	4.3	4.3	4.1	4.1	4.1
392	Careers advisers and vocational guidance specialists	4.1	4.3	4.3	4.1	4.1	4.1
393	Driving instructors (excluding HGV)	9.1	8.1	9.1	12.2	10	12.2
394	Inspectors of factories, utilities and trading standards	4.1	4.1	4.1	4.1	4.1	4.1
395	Other statutory and similar inspectors n.e.c.	4.1	4.1	4.1	4.1	4.1	4.1
396	Occupational hygienists and safety officers (health and safety)	4.1	4.3	4.3	4.1	4.1	4.1
399	Other associate professional and technical occupations n.e.c.	4.1	4.3	4.3	2	4.1	4.1
400	Civil Service administrative officers and assistants	7.1	7.1	7.1	7.1	6	7.1
401	Local government clerical officers and assistants	7.1	7.1	7.1	7.1	6	7.1
410	Accounts and wages clerks, book-keepers, other financial clerks	7.1	8.1	9.1	7.1	6	7.1
411	Counter clerks and cashiers	7.1	8.1	9.1	7.1	6	7.1
412	Debt, rent and other cash collectors	7.2	8.1	9.1	7.2	6	7.2
420	Filing, computer and other records clerks (including legal conveyancing)	7.1	8.1	9.1	7.1	6	7.1
421	Library assistants/clerks	7.1	8.1	9.1	7.1	6	7.1
430	Clerks (n.o.s.)	7.2	8.1	9.1	7.2	6	7.2
440	Stores, despatch and production control clerks	12.6	8.1	9.1	12.6	10	12.6
441	Storekeepers and warehousemen/women	13.4	8.1	9.1	12.4	10	13.4
450	Medical secretaries	7.1	8.1	9.1	7.1	6	7.1
451	Legal secretaries	7.1	8.1	9.1	7.1	6	7.1
452	Typists and word processor operators	7.1	8.1	9.1	7.1	6	7.1
459	Other secretaries, personal assistants, typists, word processor operators n.e.c.	7.1	8.1	9.1	7.1	6	7.1
460	Receptionists	12.6	8.1	9.1	12.6	10	12.6
461	Receptionist/telephonists	12.6	8.1	9.1	12.6	10	12.6
462	Telephone operators	12.6	8.1	9.1	12.6	10	12.6
463	Radio and telegraph operators, other office communication system operators	11.1	8.1	9.1	11.1	10	11.1
490	Computer operators, data processing operators, other office machine operators	7.1	8.1	9.1	7.1	6	7.1
491	Tracers, drawing office assistants	7.3	8.1	9.1	7.3	6	7.3
500	Bricklayers, masons	9.1	8.1	9.1	13.3	10	13.3
501	Roofers, slaters, tilers, sheeters, cladders	9.1	8.1	9.1	13.2	10	13.2
502	Plasterers	9.1	8.1	9.1	13.3	10	13.3
503	Glaziers	13.2	8.1	9.1	13.2	10	13.2
504	Builders, building contractors	9.1	8.1	9.1	12.4	10	12.4
505	Scaffolders, stagers, steeplejacks, riggers	12.4	8.1	9.1	12.4	10	12.4
506	Floorers, floor coverers, carpet fitters and planners, floor and wall tilers	9.1	8.1	9.1	13.3	10	13.3
507	Painters and decorators	9.1	8.1	9.1	13.3	10	13.3
509	Other construction trades n.e.c.	9.1	8.1	9.1	12.4	10	12.4
510	Centre, capstan, turret and other lathe setters and setter-operators	12.3	8.1	9.1	12.3	10	12.3
511	Boring and drilling machine setters and setter-operators	12.3	8.1	9.1	12.3	10	12.3
512	Grinding machine setters and setter-operators	12.3	8.1	9.1	12.3	10	12.3
513	Milling machine setters and setter-operators	12.3	8.1	9.1	12.3	10	12.3
514	Press setters and setter-operators	10	8.1	9.1	12.3	10	12.3
515	Tool makers, tool fitters and markers-out	11.1	8.1	9.1	11.1	10	11.1
516	Metal working production and maintenance fitters	11.1	8.1	9.1	10	10	11.1

Please note: This derivation table has no empty cells. See key at the end of table.

Table 16 - *continued*

Standard Occupational Classification 1990 unit group		Simplified NS-SEC	Employment status				
			1 Employers	2 Self-employed - no employees	3 Managers	4 Supervisors	5 Other employees
517	Precision instrument makers and repairers	11.1	8.1	9.1	11.1	10	11.1
518	Goldsmiths, silversmiths, precious stone workers	11.1	8.1	9.1	11.1	10	11.1
519	Other machine tool setters and setter-operators n.e.c. (including CNC setter-operators)	12.3	8.1	9.1	12.3	10	12.3
520	Production fitters (electrical/electronic)	11.1	8.1	9.1	11.1	10	11.1
521	Electricians, electrical maintenance fitters	11.1	8.1	9.1	11.1	10	11.1
522	Electrical engineers (not professional)	11.1	8.1	9.1	11.1	10	11.1
523	Telephone fitters	7.4	8.1	9.1	7.4	6	7.4
524	Cable jointers, lines repairers	11.1	8.1	9.1	11.1	10	11.1
525	Radio, TV and video engineers	11.1	8.1	9.1	11.1	10	11.1
526	Computer engineers, installation and maintenance	7.4	8.1	9.1	7.4	6	7.4
529	Other electrical/electronic trades n.e.c.	7.4	8.1	9.1	7.4	6	7.4
530	Smiths and forge workers	13.3	8.1	9.1	13.3	10	13.3
531	Moulders, core makers, die casters	12.3	8.1	9.1	12.3	10	12.3
532	Plumbers, heating and ventilating engineers and related trades	11.1	8.1	9.1	10	10	11.1
533	Sheet metal workers	12.3	8.1	9.1	12.3	10	12.3
534	Metal plate workers, shipwrights, riveters	13.3	8.1	9.1	13.3	10	13.3
535	Steel erectors	12.3	8.1	9.1	12.3	10	12.3
536	Barbenders, steel fixers	9.1	8.1	9.1	12.4	10	12.4
537	Welding trades	13.3	8.1	9.1	13.3	10	13.3
540	Motor mechanics, auto engineers (including road patrol engineers)	11.1	8.1	9.1	11.1	10	11.1
541	Coach and vehicle body builders	11.1	8.1	9.1	11.1	10	11.1
542	Vehicle body repairers, panel beaters	11.1	8.1	9.1	11.1	10	11.1
543	Auto electricians	11.1	8.1	9.1	11.1	10	11.1
544	Tyre and exhaust fitters	12.4	8.1	9.1	12.4	10	12.4
550	Weavers	13.3	8.1	9.1	13.3	10	13.3
551	Knitters	13.3	8.1	9.1	13.3	10	13.3
552	Warp preparers, bleachers, dyers and finishers	13.2	8.1	9.1	13.2	10	13.2
553	Sewing machinists, menders, darners and embroiderers	13.2	8.1	9.1	13.2	10	13.2
554	Coach trimmers, upholsterers and mattress makers	13.3	8.1	9.1	13.3	10	13.3
555	Shoe repairers, leather cutters and sewers, footwear lasters, makers and finishers, other leather making and repairing	13.3	8.1	9.1	13.3	10	13.3
556	Tailors and dressmakers	9.1	8.1	9.1	12.3	10	12.3
557	Clothing cutters, milliners, furriers	12.3	8.1	9.1	12.3	10	12.3
559	Other textiles, garments and related trades n.e.c.	13.3	8.1	9.1	13.3	10	13.3
560	Originators, compositors and print preparers	11.1	8.1	9.1	11.1	10	11.1
561	Printers	11.1	8.1	9.1	11.1	10	11.1
562	Bookbinders and print finishers	13.3	8.1	9.1	13.3	10	13.3
563	Screen printers	11.1	8.1	9.1	11.1	10	11.1
569	Other printing and related trades n.e.c.	11.1	8.1	9.1	11.1	10	11.1
570	Carpenters and joiners	9.1	8.1	9.1	13.3	10	13.3
571	Cabinet makers	13.3	8.1	9.1	13.3	10	13.3
572	Case and box makers	12.3	8.1	9.1	12.3	10	12.3
573	Pattern makers (moulds)	11.1	8.1	9.1	11.1	10	11.1
579	Other woodworking trades n.e.c.	9.1	8.1	9.1	13.3	10	13.3
580	Bakers, flour confectioners	11.1	8.1	9.1	11.1	10	11.1
581	Butchers, meat cutters	13.3	8.1	9.1	13.3	10	13.3
582	Fishmongers, poultry dressers	13.3	8.1	9.1	13.3	10	13.3
590	Glass product and ceramics makers	13.3	8.1	9.1	13.3	10	13.3
591	Glass product and ceramics finishers and decorators	13.3	8.1	9.1	13.3	10	13.3
592	Dental technicians	7.3	8.1	9.1	7.3	6	7.3
593	Musical instrument makers, piano tuners	9.1	8.1	9.1	11.1	10	11.1
594	Gardeners, groundsmen/groundswomen	11.1	8.1	9.1	11.1	10	11.1
595	Horticultural trades	12.5	8.2	9.2	12.5	10	12.5
596	Coach painters, other spray painters	12.3	8.1	9.1	12.3	10	12.3
597	Face trained coalmining workers, shotfirers and deputies	13.3	8.1	9.1	13.3	10	13.3
598	Office machinery mechanics	7.4	8.1	9.1	7.4	6	7.4
599	Other craft and related occupations n.e.c.	11.1	8.1	9.1	11.1	10	11.1
600	NCOs and other ranks, UK armed forces	7.2	7.2	7.2	7.2	6	7.2
601	NCOs and other ranks, foreign and Commonwealth armed forces	7.2	7.2	7.2	7.2	6	7.2
610	Police officers (sergeant and below)	7.2	7.2	7.2	7.2	6	7.2
611	Fire service officers (leading fire officer and below)	7.2	7.2	7.2	7.2	6	7.2
612	Prison service officers (below principal officer)	7.2	7.2	7.2	7.2	6	7.2

Please note: This derivation table has no empty cells. See key at the end of table.

Table 16 - *continued*

Standard Occupational Classification 990 unit group		Simplified NS-SEC	Employment status				
			1 Employers	2 Self-employed - no employees	3 Managers	4 Supervisors	5 Other employees
613	Customs and excise officers, immigration officers (customs: below chief preventive officer; excise: below surveyor)	4.1	4.1	4.1	4.1	4.1	4.1
614	Traffic wardens	12.2	12.2	12.2	12.2	10	12.2
615	Security guards and related occupations	12.2	8.1	9.1	5	10	12.2
619	Other security and protective service occupations n.e.c.	13.1	8.1	9.1	13.1	10	13.1
620	Chefs, cooks	12.2	8.1	9.1	10	10	12.2
621	Waiters, waitresses	13.1	8.1	9.1	13.1	10	13.1
622	Bar staff	13.1	8.1	9.1	13.1	10	13.1
630	Travel and flight attendants	13.1	8.1	9.1	13.1	6	13.1
631	Railway station staff	11.2	8.1	9.1	11.2	10	11.2
640	Assistant nurses, nursing auxiliaries	7.3	8.1	9.1	7.3	6	7.3
641	Hospital ward assistants	7.3	8.1	9.1	7.3	6	7.3
642	Ambulance staff	7.2	7.2	7.2	7.2	6	7.2
643	Dental nurses	12.2	8.1	9.1	12.2	10	12.2
644	Care assistants and attendants	12.2	8.1	9.1	12.2	10	12.2
650	Nursery nurses	7.2	8.1	9.1	7.2	6	7.2
651	Playgroup leaders	12.7	8.1	9.1	12.7	10	12.7
652	Educational assistants	12.7	8.1	9.1	12.7	10	12.7
659	Other childcare and related occupations n.e.c.	13.1	8.1	9.1	13.1	10	13.1
660	Hairdressers, barbers	13.1	8.1	9.1	13.1	10	13.1
661	Beauticians and related occupations	9.1	8.1	9.1	12.2	10	12.2
670	Domestic housekeepers and related occupations	12.2	8.1	9.1	12.2	10	12.2
671	Housekeepers (non-domestic)	10	8.1	9.1	12.2	10	12.2
672	Caretakers	12.2	8.1	9.1	12.2	10	12.2
673	Launderers, dry cleaners, pressers	13.2	8.1	9.1	13.2	10	13.2
690	Undertakers	12.2	8.1	9.1	12.2	10	12.2
691	Bookmakers	5	8.1	9.1	5	10	12.2
699	Other personal and protective service occupations n.e.c.	12.2	8.1	9.1	12.2	10	12.2
700	Buyers (retail trade)	4.1	4.3	4.3	4.1	4.1	4.1
701	Buyers and purchasing officers (not retail)	4.1	4.3	4.3	4.1	4.1	4.1
702	Importers and exporters	4.2	4.4	4.4	4.2	4.2	4.2
703	Air, commodity and ship brokers	3.2	3.4	3.4	3.2	3.2	3.2
710	Technical and wholesale sales representatives	4.2	4.4	4.4	5	4.2	4.2
719	Other sales representatives n.e.c.	7.2	4.4	4.4	4.2	6	7.2
720	Sales assistants	12.1	8.1	9.1	12.1	10	12.1
721	Retail cash desk and check-out operators	12.1	8.1	9.1	12.1	10	12.1
722	Petrol pump forecourt attendants	12.1	8.1	9.1	12.1	10	12.1
730	Collector salespersons and credit agents	9.1	8.1	9.1	12.1	10	12.1
731	Roundsmen/women and van salespersons	13.3	8.1	9.1	13.3	10	13.3
732	Market and street traders and assistants	9.1	8.1	9.1	13.1	10	13.1
733	Scrap dealers, scrap metal merchants	9.1	8.1	9.1	5	5	5
790	Merchandisers	7.2	8.1	9.1	7.2	6	7.2
791	Window dressers, floral arrangers	13.1	8.1	9.1	13.1	10	13.1
792	Telephone salespersons	12.1	8.1	9.1	12.1	10	12.1
800	Bakery and confectionery process operatives	12.4	8.1	9.1	12.4	10	12.4
801	Brewery and vinery process operatives	12.4	8.1	9.1	12.4	10	12.4
802	Tobacco process operatives	12.4	8.1	9.1	12.4	10	12.4
809	Other food, drink and tobacco process operatives n.e.c.	12.4	8.1	9.1	12.4	10	12.4
810	Tannery production operatives	11.2	8.1	9.1	11.2	10	11.2
811	Preparatory fibre processors	13.2	8.1	9.1	13.2	10	13.2
812	Spinners, doublers, twisters	13.2	8.1	9.1	13.2	10	13.2
813	Winders, reelers	13.2	8.1	9.1	13.2	10	13.2
814	Other textiles processing operatives	13.2	8.1	9.1	13.2	10	13.2
820	Chemical, gas and petroleum process plant operatives	11.2	8.1	9.1	11.2	10	11.2
821	Paper, wood and related process plant operatives	12.3	8.1	9.1	12.3	10	12.3
822	Cutting and slitting machine operatives (paper products etc)	12.3	8.1	9.1	12.3	10	12.3
823	Glass and ceramics furnace operatives, kilnsetters	12.3	8.1	9.1	12.3	10	12.3
824	Rubber process operatives, moulding machine operatives, tyre builders	12.3	8.1	9.1	12.3	10	12.3
825	Plastics process operatives, moulders and extruders	12.4	8.1	9.1	12.4	10	12.4
826	Synthetic fibre makers	11.2	8.1	9.1	11.2	10	11.2
829	Other chemicals, paper, plastics and related process operatives n.e.c.	12.3	8.1	9.1	12.3	10	12.3
830	Furnace operatives (metal)	12.3	8.1	9.1	12.3	10	12.3
831	Metal drawers	12.3	8.1	9.1	12.3	10	12.3
832	Rollers	12.3	8.1	9.1	12.3	10	12.3

Please note: This derivation table has no empty cells. See key at the end of table.

Table 16 - *continued*

Standard Occupational Classification 1990 unit group		Simplified NS-SEC	Employment status				
			1 Employers	2 Self-employed - no employees	3 Managers	4 Supervisors	5 Other employees
833	Annealers, hardeners, temperers (metal)	12.3	8.1	9.1	12.3	10	12.3
834	Electroplaters, galvanisers, colour coaters	12.3	8.1	9.1	12.3	10	12.3
839	Other metal making and treating process operatives n.e.c.	12.3	8.1	9.1	12.3	10	12.3
840	Machine tool operatives (including CNC machine tool operatives)	12.4	8.1	9.1	12.4	10	12.4
841	Press stamping and automatic machine operatives	12.4	8.1	9.1	12.4	10	12.4
842	Metal polishers	12.4	8.1	9.1	12.4	10	12.4
843	Metal dressing operatives	12.4	8.1	9.1	12.4	10	12.4
844	Shot blasters	12.4	8.1	9.1	12.4	10	12.4
850	Assemblers/lineworkers (electrical/electronic goods)	12.4	8.1	9.1	12.4	10	12.4
851	Assemblers/lineworkers (vehicles and other metal goods)	12.4	8.1	9.1	12.4	10	12.4
859	Other assemblers/lineworkers n.e.c.	13.2	8.1	9.1	13.2	10	13.2
860	Inspectors, viewers and testers (metal and electrical goods)	11.2	8.1	9.1	11.2	10	11.2
861	Inspectors, viewers, testers and examiners (other manufactured goods)	11.2	8.1	9.1	11.2	10	11.2
862	Packers, bottlers, canners, fillers	13.2	8.1	9.1	13.2	10	13.2
863	Weighers, graders, sorters	13.2	8.1	9.1	13.2	10	13.2
864	Routine laboratory testers	7.3	8.1	9.1	7.3	6	7.3
869	Other routine process operatives n.e.c.	11.2	8.1	9.1	11.2	10	11.2
870	Bus inspectors	10	8.1	9.1	11.2	10	11.2
871	Road transport depot inspectors and related occupations	10	8.1	9.1	11.2	10	11.2
872	Drivers of road goods vehicles	13.3	8.1	9.1	13.3	10	13.3
873	Bus and coach drivers	13.3	8.1	9.1	13.3	10	13.3
874	Taxi, cab drivers and chauffeurs	9.1	8.1	9.1	13.3	10	13.3
875	Bus conductors	13.3	8.1	9.1	13.3	10	13.3
880	Seafarers (merchant navy); barge, lighter and boat operatives	12.4	8.1	9.1	12.4	10	12.4
881	Rail transport inspectors, supervisors and guards	11.2	8.1	9.1	11.2	10	11.2
882	Rail engine drivers and assistants	11.2	11.2	11.2	11.2	10	11.2
883	Rail signal operatives and crossing keepers	11.2	8.1	9.1	11.2	10	11.2
884	Shunters and points operatives	11.2	8.1	9.1	11.2	10	11.2
885	Mechanical plant drivers and operatives (earth moving and civil engineering)	13.3	8.1	9.1	13.3	10	13.3
886	Crane drivers	12.3	8.1	9.1	12.3	10	12.3
887	Fork lift and mechanical truck drivers	12.3	8.1	9.1	12.3	10	12.3
889	Other transport and machinery operatives n.e.c.	13.4	8.1	9.1	13.4	10	13.4
890	Washers, screeners and crushers in mines and quarries	11.2	8.1	9.1	11.2	10	11.2
891	Printing machine minders and assistants	12.3	8.1	9.1	12.3	10	12.3
892	Water and sewerage plant attendants	11.2	8.1	9.1	11.2	10	11.2
893	Electrical, energy, boiler and related plant operatives and attendants	12.4	8.1	9.1	12.4	10	12.4
894	Oilers, greasers, lubricators	12.4	8.1	9.1	12.4	10	12.4
895	Mains and service pipe layers, pipe jointers	13.4	8.1	9.1	13.4	10	13.4
896	Construction and related operatives	10	8.1	9.1	10	10	13.4
897	Woodworking machine operatives	12.3	8.1	9.1	12.3	10	12.3
898	Mine (excluding coal) and quarry workers	11.2	8.1	9.1	11.2	10	11.2
899	Other plant and machine operatives n.e.c.	12.4	8.1	9.1	10	10	12.4
900	Farm workers	12.5	8.2	9.2	12.5	6	12.5
901	Agricultural machinery drivers and operatives	12.5	8.2	9.2	12.5	10	12.5
902	All other occupations in farming and related	13.5	8.2	9.2	13.5	10	13.5
903	Fishing and related workers	9.1	8.1	9.1	13.5	10	13.5
904	Forestry workers	9.2	8.2	9.2	12.5	10	12.5
910	Coal mine labourers	13.3	8.1	9.1	13.3	10	13.3
911	Labourers in foundries	13.4	8.1	9.1	13.4	10	13.4
912	Labourers in engineering and allied trades	13.4	8.1	9.1	13.4	10	13.4
913	Mates to metal/electrical and related fitters	13.4	8.1	9.1	13.4	10	13.4
919	Other labourers in making and processing industries n.e.c.	13.4	8.1	9.1	13.4	10	13.4
920	Mates to woodworking trades workers	13.4	8.1	9.1	13.4	10	13.4
921	Mates to building trades workers	9.1	8.1	9.1	13.4	10	13.4
922	Rail construction and maintenance workers	11.2	8.1	9.1	11.2	10	11.2
923	Road construction and maintenance workers	10	8.1	9.1	12.4	10	12.4
924	Paviors, kerb layers	9.1	8.1	9.1	12.4	10	12.4
929	Other building and civil engineering labourers n.e.c.	13.4	8.1	9.1	13.4	10	13.4
930	Stevedores, dockers	13.4	8.1	9.1	13.4	10	13.4
931	Goods porters	13.4	8.1	9.1	12.4	10	13.4

Please note: This derivation table has no empty cells. See key at the end of table.

Table 16 - *continued*

Standard Occupational Classification 1990 unit group		Simplified NS-SEC	Employment status				
			1 Employers	2 Self-employed - no employees	3 Managers	4 Supervisors	5 Other employees
932	Slingers	13.4	8.1	9.1	13.4	10	13.4
933	Refuse and salvage collectors	13.4	8.1	9.1	13.4	10	13.4
934	Driver's mates	13.4	8.1	9.1	13.4	10	13.4
940	Postal workers, mail sorters	12.2	8.1	9.1	12.2	10	12.2
941	Messengers, couriers	12.2	8.1	9.1	12.2	10	12.2
950	Hospital porters	12.2	8.1	9.1	12.2	10	12.2
951	Hotel porters	13.1	8.1	9.1	13.1	10	13.1
952	Kitchen porters, hands	12.2	8.1	9.1	12.2	10	12.2
953	Counterhands, catering assistants	12.2	8.1	9.1	12.2	10	12.2
954	Shelf fillers	12.1	8.1	9.1	12.1	10	12.1
955	Lift and car park attendants	13.4	8.1	9.1	13.4	10	13.4
956	Window cleaners	9.1	8.1	9.1	13.2	10	13.2
957	Road sweepers	13.4	8.1	9.1	13.4	10	13.4
958	Cleaners, domestics	13.4	8.1	9.1	13.4	10	13.4
959	Other occupations in sales and services n.e.c.	13.4	8.1	9.1	13.4	10	13.4
990	All other labourers and related workers	13.4	8.1	9.1	13.4	10	13.4
999	All others in miscellaneous occupations n.e.c.	13.1	8.1	9.1	13.1	10	13.1

Please note: This derivation table has no empty cells.

Cells filled by the developers in April 2001.

Cells filled by using the priority order rules (see Appendix A).

Table **17**

NS-SEC based on SOC90 simplified and reduced derivation table: analytic classes

Standard Occupational Classification 1990 unit group		Simplified NS-SEC	Employment status				
			1 Employers	2 Self-employed - no employees	3 Managers	4 Supervisors	5 Other employees
100	General administrators; national government (Assistant Secretary/Grade 5 and above)	1.1	1.1	1.1	1.1	1.1	1.1
101	General managers; large companies and organisations	1.1	1.1	1.1	1.1	1.1	1.1
102	Local government officers (administrative and executive functions)	1.1	4	4	1.1	1.1	1.1
103	General administrators; national government (HEO to Senior Principal/Grade 6)	2	2	2	2	2	2
110	Production, works and maintenance managers	1.1	4	4	1.1	2	1.1
111	Managers in building and contracting	2	4	4	2	2	2
112	Clerks of works	2	4	4	2	2	2
113	Managers in mining and energy industries	1.1	4	4	1.1	1.1	1.1
120	Treasurers and company financial managers	1.1	1.2	1.2	1.1	1.1	1.1
121	Marketing and sales managers	1.1	4	2	1.1	1.1	1.1
122	Purchasing managers	1.1	4	4	1.1	1.1	1.1
123	Advertising and public relations managers	1.1	4	2	1.1	1.1	1.1
124	Personnel, training and industrial relations managers	1.1	4	4	1.1	1.1	1.1
125	Organisation and methods and work study managers	1.1	4	4	1.1	1.1	1.1
126	Computer systems and data processing managers	1.1	4	4	1.1	1.1	1.1
127	Company secretaries	3	4	4	3	2	3
130	Credit controllers	3	4	4	3	2	3
131	Bank, Building Society and Post Office managers (except self-employed)	2	4	4	2	2	2
132	Civil Service executive officers	2	2	2	2	2	2
139	Other financial institution and office managers n.e.c.	2	4	4	2	2	2
140	Transport managers	2	4	4	2	2	2
141	Stores controllers	6	4	4	6	6	6
142	Managers in warehousing and other materials handling	2	4	4	2	2	2
150	Officers in UK armed forces	1.1	1.1	1.1	1.1	1.1	1.1
151	Officers in foreign and Commonwealth armed forces	1.1	1.1	1.1	1.1	1.1	1.1
152	Police officers (inspector and above)	1.1	1.1	1.1	1.1	1.1	1.1
153	Fire service officers (station officer and above)	1.1	1.1	1.1	1.1	1.1	1.1
154	Prison officers (principal officer and above)	1.1	1.1	1.1	1.1	1.1	1.1
155	Customs and excise, immigration service officers (customs: chief preventive officer and above; excise: surveyor and above)	1.1	1.1	1.1	1.1	1.1	1.1
160	Farm owners and managers, horticulturists	4	4	4	2	2	2
169	Other managers in farming, horticulture, forestry and fishing n.e.c.	4	4	4	5	5	5
170	Property and estate managers	2	4	4	2	2	2
171	Garage managers and proprietors	4	4	4	2	2	2
172	Hairdressers' and barbers' managers and proprietors	4	4	4	2	2	2
173	Hotel and accommodation managers	4	4	4	2	2	2
174	Restaurant and catering managers	2	4	4	2	2	2
175	Publicans, innkeepers and club stewards	2	4	4	2	2	2
176	Entertainment and sports managers	2	4	4	2	2	2
177	Travel agency managers	2	4	4	2	2	2
178	Managers and proprietors of butchers and fishmongers	4	4	4	2	2	2
179	Managers and proprietors in service industries n.e.c.	2	4	4	2	2	2
190	Officials of trade associations, trade unions, professional bodies and charities	2	4	4	2	2	2
191	Registrars and administrators of educational establishments	1.2	1.2	1.2	1.2	1.2	1.2
199	Other managers and administrators n.e.c.	2	4	4	2	2	2
200	Chemists	1.2	1.2	1.2	2	1.2	1.2
201	Biological scientists and biochemists	1.2	1.2	1.2	2	1.2	1.2
202	Physicists, geologists and meteorologists	1.2	1.2	1.2	2	1.2	1.2
209	Other natural scientists n.e.c.	1.2	1.2	1.2	1.2	1.2	1.2

Please note: This derivation table has no empty cells. See key at the end of table.

Table 17 - *continued*

Standard Occupational Classification 990 unit group		Simplified NS-SEC	Employment status				
			1 Employers	2 Self-employed - no employees	3 Managers	4 Supervisors	5 Other employees
210	Civil, structural, municipal, mining and quarrying engineers	1.2	1.2	1.2	1.2	1.2	1.2
211	Mechanical engineers	1.2	1.2	1.2	1.2	1.2	1.2
212	Electrical engineers	1.2	1.2	1.2	1.2	1.2	1.2
213	Electronic engineers	1.2	1.2	1.2	1.2	1.2	1.2
214	Software engineers	1.2	1.2	1.2	1.2	1.2	1.2
215	Chemical engineers	1.2	1.2	1.2	1.2	1.2	1.2
216	Design and development engineers	1.2	1.2	1.2	1.2	1.2	1.2
217	Process and production engineers	2	2	2	2	2	2
218	Planning and quality control engineers	2	2	2	2	2	2
219	Other engineers and technologists n.e.c.	1.2	1.2	1.2	1.2	1.2	1.2
220	Medical practitioners	1.2	1.2	1.2	1.2	1.2	1.2
221	Pharmacists/pharmacologists	1.2	1.2	1.2	2	1.2	1.2
222	Ophthalmic opticians	2	2	2	2	2	2
223	Dental practitioners	1.2	1.2	1.2	1.2	1.2	1.2
224	Veterinarians	1.2	1.2	1.2	1.2	1.2	1.2
230	University and polytechnic teaching professionals	1.2	1.2	1.2	1.2	1.2	1.2
231	Higher and further education teaching professionals	2	2	2	2	2	2
232	Education officers, school inspectors	1.2	1.2	1.2	1.2	1.2	1.2
233	Secondary (and middle school deemed secondary) education teaching professionals	2	2	2	2	2	2
234	Primary (and middle school deemed primary) and nursery education teaching professionals	2	2	2	2	2	2
235	Special education teaching professionals	2	2	2	2	2	2
239	Other teaching professionals n.e.c.	4	4	4	3	2	3
240	Judges and officers of the Court	1.2	1.2	1.2	1.2	1.2	1.2
241	Barristers and advocates	1.2	1.2	1.2	1.2	1.2	1.2
242	Solicitors	1.2	1.2	1.2	1.2	1.2	1.2
250	Chartered and certified accountants	1.2	1.2	1.2	1.2	1.2	1.2
251	Management accountants	1.2	1.2	1.2	1.2	1.2	1.2
252	Actuaries, economists and statisticians	1.2	1.2	1.2	1.2	1.2	1.2
253	Management consultants, business analysts	1.2	1.2	1.2	1.2	1.2	1.2
260	Architects	1.2	1.2	1.2	1.2	1.2	1.2
261	Town planners	1.2	1.2	1.2	1.2	1.2	1.2
262	Building, land, mining and 'general practice' surveyors	1.2	1.2	1.2	1.2	1.2	1.2
270	Librarians	2	2	2	2	2	2
271	Archivists and curators	2	2	2	2	2	2
290	Psychologists	1.2	1.2	1.2	1.2	1.2	1.2
291	Other social and behavioural scientists	1.2	1.2	1.2	1.2	1.2	1.2
292	Clergy	1.2	1.2	1.2	1.2	1.2	1.2
293	Social workers, probation officers	2	2	2	2	2	2
300	Laboratory technicians	2	2	2	2	2	2
301	Engineering technicians	2	2	2	2	2	2
302	Electrical/electronic technicians	3	4	4	3	2	3
303	Architectural and town planning technicians	2	2	2	2	2	2
304	Building and civil engineering technicians	2	2	2	2	2	2
309	Other scientific technicians n.e.c.	2	2	2	2	2	2
310	Draughtspersons	3	4	4	3	2	3
311	Building inspectors	2	2	2	2	2	2
312	Quantity surveyors	2	2	2	2	2	2
313	Marine, insurance and other surveyors	2	1.2	1.2	2	1.2	2
320	Computer analyst/programmers	1.2	1.2	1.2	1.2	1.2	1.2
330	Air traffic planners and controllers	2	2	2	2	2	2
331	Aircraft flight deck officers	1.2	1.2	1.2	1.2	1.2	1.2
332	Ship and hovercraft officers	2	2	2	2	2	2
340	Nurses	2	4	2	2	2	2
341	Midwives	2	2	2	2	2	2
342	Medical radiographers	2	2	2	2	2	2
343	Physiotherapists	2	2	2	2	2	2
344	Chiropodists	2	2	2	2	2	2
345	Dispensing opticians	3	4	4	3	2	3
346	Medical technicians, dental auxiliaries	6	4	4	3	5	6
347	Occupational and speech therapists, psychotherapists, therapists n.e.c.	2	2	2	2	2	2
348	Environmental health officers	1.2	1.2	1.2	1.2	1.2	1.2
349	Other health associate professionals n.e.c.	6	4	4	6	5	6
350	Legal service and related occupations	3	1.2	4	3	2	3
360	Estimators, valuers	2	2	2	2	2	2
361	Underwriters, claims assessors, brokers, investment analysts	2	2	2	1.2	2	2

Please note: This derivation table has no empty cells. See key at the end of table.

Table 17 - *continued*

Standard Occupational Classification 1990 unit group		Simplified NS-SEC	Employment status				
			1 Employers	2 Self-employed - no employees	3 Managers	4 Supervisors	5 Other employees
362	Taxation experts	1.2	1.2	1.2	1.2	1.2	1.2
363	Personnel and industrial relations officers	2	2	2	2	2	2
364	Organisation and methods and work study officers	1.2	1.2	1.2	1.2	1.2	1.2
370	Matrons, houseparents	6	4	4	5	5	6
371	Welfare, community and youth workers	2	2	2	2	2	2
380	Authors, writers, journalists	2	2	2	2	2	2
381	Artists, commercial artists, graphic designers	4	4	4	3	2	3
382	Industrial designers	4	4	4	2	2	3
383	Clothing designers	3	4	4	2	2	3
384	Actors, entertainers, stage managers, producers and directors	2	2	2	2	2	2
385	Musicians	2	2	2	2	2	2
386	Photographers, camera, sound and video equipment operators	3	4	4	3	2	3
387	Professional athletes, sports officials	2	2	2	2	2	2
390	Information officers	2	2	2	2	2	2
391	Vocational and industrial trainers	2	2	2	2	2	2
392	Careers advisers and vocational guidance specialists	2	2	2	2	2	2
393	Driving instructors (excluding HGV)	4	4	4	6	5	6
394	Inspectors of factories, utilities and trading standards	2	2	2	2	2	2
395	Other statutory and similar inspectors n.e.c.	2	2	2	2	2	2
396	Occupational hygienists and safety officers (health and safety)	2	2	2	2	2	2
399	Other associate professional and technical occupations n.e.c.	2	2	2	1.1	2	2
400	Civil Service administrative officers and assistants	3	3	3	3	2	3
401	Local government clerical officers and assistants	3	3	3	3	2	3
410	Accounts and wages clerks, book-keepers, other financial clerks	3	4	4	3	2	3
411	Counter clerks and cashiers	3	4	4	3	2	3
412	Debt, rent and other cash collectors	3	4	4	3	2	3
420	Filing, computer and other records clerks (including legal conveyancing)	3	4	4	3	2	3
421	Library assistants/clerks	3	4	4	3	2	3
430	Clerks (n.o.s.)	3	4	4	3	2	3
440	Stores, despatch and production control clerks	6	4	4	6	5	6
441	Storekeepers and warehousemen/women	7	4	4	6	5	7
450	Medical secretaries	3	4	4	3	2	3
451	Legal secretaries	3	4	4	3	2	3
452	Typists and word processor operators	3	4	4	3	2	3
459	Other secretaries, personal assistants, typists, word processor operators n.e.c.	3	4	4	3	2	3
460	Receptionists	6	4	4	6	5	6
461	Receptionist/telephonists	6	4	4	6	5	6
462	Telephone operators	6	4	4	6	5	6
463	Radio and telegraph operators, other office communication system operators	5	4	4	5	5	5
490	Computer operators, data processing operators, other office machine operators	3	4	4	3	2	3
491	Tracers, drawing office assistants	3	4	4	3	2	3
500	Bricklayers, masons	4	4	4	7	5	7
501	Roofers, slaters, tilers, sheeters, cladders	4	4	4	7	5	7
502	Plasterers	4	4	4	7	5	7
503	Glaziers	7	4	4	7	5	7
504	Builders, building contractors	4	4	4	6	5	6
505	Scaffolders, stagers, steeplejacks, riggers	6	4	4	6	5	6
506	Floorers, floor coverers, carpet fitters and planners, floor and wall tilers	4	4	4	7	5	7
507	Painters and decorators	4	4	4	7	5	7
509	Other construction trades n.e.c.	4	4	4	6	5	6
510	Centre, capstan, turret and other lathe setters and setter-operators	6	4	4	6	5	6
511	Boring and drilling machine setters and setter-operators	6	4	4	6	5	6
512	Grinding machine setters and setter-operators	6	4	4	6	5	6
513	Milling machine setters and setter-operators	6	4	4	6	5	6
514	Press setters and setter-operators	5	4	4	6	5	6
515	Tool makers, tool fitters and markers-out	5	4	4	5	5	5
516	Metal working production and maintenance fitters	5	4	4	5	5	5

Please note: This derivation table has no empty cells. See key at the end of table.

Table 17 - *continued*

Standard Occupational Classification 1990 unit group		Simplified NS-SEC	Employment status				
			1 Employers	2 Self-employed - no employees	3 Managers	4 Supervisors	5 Other employees
517	Precision instrument makers and repairers	5	4	4	5	5	5
518	Goldsmiths, silversmiths, precious stone workers	5	4	4	5	5	5
519	Other machine tool setters and setter-operators n.e.c. (including CNC setter-operators)	6	4	4	6	5	6
520	Production fitters (electrical/electronic)	5	4	4	5	5	5
521	Electricians, electrical maintenance fitters	5	4	4	5	5	5
522	Electrical engineers (not professional)	5	4	4	5	5	5
523	Telephone fitters	3	4	4	3	2	3
524	Cable jointers, lines repairers	5	4	4	5	5	5
525	Radio, TV and video engineers	5	4	4	5	5	5
526	Computer engineers, installation and maintenance	3	4	4	3	2	3
529	Other electrical/electronic trades n.e.c.	3	4	4	3	2	3
530	Smiths and forge workers	7	4	4	7	5	7
531	Moulders, core makers, die casters	6	4	4	6	5	6
532	Plumbers, heating and ventilating engineers and related trades	5	4	4	5	5	5
533	Sheet metal workers	6	4	4	6	5	6
534	Metal plate workers, shipwrights, riveters	7	4	4	7	5	7
535	Steel erectors	6	4	4	6	5	6
536	Barbenders, steel fixers	4	4	4	6	5	6
537	Welding trades	7	4	4	7	5	7
540	Motor mechanics, auto engineers (including road patrol engineers)	5	4	4	5	5	5
541	Coach and vehicle body builders	5	4	4	5	5	5
542	Vehicle body repairers, panel beaters	5	4	4	5	5	5
543	Auto electricians	5	4	4	5	5	5
544	Tyre and exhaust fitters	6	4	4	6	5	6
550	Weavers	7	4	4	7	5	7
551	Knitters	7	4	4	7	5	7
552	Warp preparers, bleachers, dyers and finishers	7	4	4	7	5	7
553	Sewing machinists, menders, darners and embroiderers	7	4	4	7	5	7
554	Coach trimmers, upholsterers and mattress makers	7	4	4	7	5	7
555	Shoe repairers, leather cutters and sewers, footwear lasters, makers and finishers, other leather making and repairing	7	4	4	7	5	7
556	Tailors and dressmakers	4	4	4	6	5	6
557	Clothing cutters, milliners, furriers	6	4	4	6	5	6
559	Other textiles, garments and related trades n.e.c.	7	4	4	7	5	7
560	Originators, compositors and print preparers	5	4	4	5	5	5
561	Printers	5	4	4	5	5	5
562	Bookbinders and print finishers	7	4	4	7	5	7
563	Screen printers	5	4	4	5	5	5
569	Other printing and related trades n.e.c.	5	4	4	5	5	5
570	Carpenters and joiners	4	4	4	7	5	7
571	Cabinet makers	7	4	4	7	5	7
572	Case and box makers	6	4	4	6	5	6
573	Pattern makers (moulds)	5	4	4	5	5	5
579	Other woodworking trades n.e.c.	4	4	4	7	5	7
580	Bakers, flour confectioners	5	4	4	5	5	5
581	Butchers, meat cutters	7	4	4	7	5	7
582	Fishmongers, poultry dressers	7	4	4	7	5	7
590	Glass product and ceramics makers	7	4	4	7	5	7
591	Glass product and ceramics finishers and decorators	7	4	4	7	5	7
592	Dental technicians	3	4	4	3	2	3
593	Musical instrument makers, piano tuners	4	4	4	5	5	5
594	Gardeners, groundsmen/groundswomen	5	4	4	5	5	5
595	Horticultural trades	6	4	4	6	5	6
596	Coach painters, other spray painters	6	4	4	6	5	6
597	Face trained coalmining workers, shotfirers and deputies	7	4	4	7	5	7
598	Office machinery mechanics	3	4	4	3	2	3
599	Other craft and related occupations n.e.c.	5	4	4	5	5	5
600	NCOs and other ranks, UK armed forces	3	3	3	3	2	3
601	NCOs and other ranks, foreign and Commonwealth armed forces	3	3	3	3	2	3
610	Police officers (sergeant and below)	3	3	3	3	2	3
611	Fire service officers (leading fire officer and below)	3	3	3	3	2	3
612	Prison service officers (below principal officer)	3	3	3	3	2	3

Please note: This derivation table has no empty cells. See key at the end of table.

Table 17 - *continued*

Standard Occupational Classification 1990 unit group		Simplified NS-SEC	Employment status				
			1 Employers	2 Self-employed - no employees	3 Managers	4 Supervisors	5 Other employees
613	Customs and excise officers, immigration officers (customs: below chief preventive officer; excise: below surveyor)	2	2	2	2	2	2
614	Traffic wardens	6	6	6	6	5	6
615	Security guards and related occupations	6	4	4	2	5	6
619	Other security and protective service occupations n.e.c.	7	4	4	7	5	7
620	Chefs, cooks	6	4	4	5	5	6
621	Waiters, waitresses	7	4	4	7	5	7
622	Bar staff	7	4	4	7	5	7
630	Travel and flight attendants	7	4	4	7	2	7
631	Railway station staff	5	4	4	5	5	5
640	Assistant nurses, nursing auxiliaries	3	4	4	3	2	3
641	Hospital ward assistants	3	4	4	3	2	3
642	Ambulance staff	3	3	3	3	2	3
643	Dental nurses	6	4	4	6	5	6
644	Care assistants and attendants	6	4	4	6	5	6
650	Nursery nurses	3	4	4	3	2	3
651	Playgroup leaders	6	4	4	6	5	6
652	Educational assistants	6	4	4	6	5	6
659	Other childcare and related occupations n.e.c.	7	4	4	7	5	7
660	Hairdressers, barbers	7	4	4	7	5	7
661	Beauticians and related occupations	4	4	4	6	5	6
670	Domestic housekeepers and related occupations	6	4	4	6	5	6
671	Housekeepers (non-domestic)	5	4	4	6	5	6
672	Caretakers	6	4	4	6	5	6
673	Launderers, dry cleaners, pressers	7	4	4	7	5	7
690	Undertakers	6	4	4	6	5	6
691	Bookmakers	2	4	4	2	5	6
699	Other personal and protective service occupations n.e.c.	6	4	4	6	5	6
700	Buyers (retail trade)	2	2	2	2	2	2
701	Buyers and purchasing officers (not retail)	2	2	2	2	2	2
702	Importers and exporters	2	2	2	2	2	2
703	Air, commodity and ship brokers	1.2	1.2	1.2	1.2	1.2	1.2
710	Technical and wholesale sales representatives	2	2	2	2	2	2
719	Other sales representatives n.e.c.	3	2	2	2	2	3
720	Sales assistants	6	4	4	6	5	6
721	Retail cash desk and check-out operators	6	4	4	6	5	6
722	Petrol pump forecourt attendants	6	4	4	6	5	6
730	Collector salespersons and credit agents	4	4	4	6	5	6
731	Roundsmen/women and van salespersons	7	4	4	7	5	7
732	Market and street traders and assistants	4	4	4	7	5	7
733	Scrap dealers, scrap metal merchants	4	4	4	2	2	2
790	Merchandisers	3	4	4	3	2	3
791	Window dressers, floral arrangers	7	4	4	7	5	7
792	Telephone salespersons	6	4	4	6	5	6
800	Bakery and confectionery process operatives	6	4	4	6	5	6
801	Brewery and vinery process operatives	6	4	4	6	5	6
802	Tobacco process operatives	6	4	4	6	5	6
809	Other food, drink and tobacco process operatives n.e.c.	6	4	4	6	5	6
810	Tannery production operatives	5	4	4	5	5	5
811	Preparatory fibre processors	7	4	4	7	5	7
812	Spinners, doublers, twisters	7	4	4	7	5	7
813	Winders, reelers	7	4	4	7	5	7
814	Other textiles processing operatives	7	4	4	7	5	7
820	Chemical, gas and petroleum process plant operatives	5	4	4	5	5	5
821	Paper, wood and related process plant operatives	6	4	4	6	5	6
822	Cutting and slitting machine operatives (paper products etc)	6	4	4	6	5	6
823	Glass and ceramics furnace operatives, kilnsetters	6	4	4	6	5	6
824	Rubber process operatives, moulding machine operatives, tyre builders	6	4	4	6	5	6
825	Plastics process operatives, moulders and extruders	6	4	4	6	5	6
826	Synthetic fibre makers	5	4	4	5	5	5
829	Other chemicals, paper, plastics and related process operatives n.e.c.	6	4	4	6	5	6
830	Furnace operatives (metal)	6	4	4	6	5	6
831	Metal drawers	6	4	4	6	5	6
832	Rollers	6	4	4	6	5	6

Please note: This derivation table has no empty cells. See key at the end of table.

Table 17 - *continued*

Standard Occupational Classification 1990 unit group		Simplified NS-SEC	Employment status				
			1 Employers	2 Self-employed - no employees	3 Managers	4 Supervisors	5 Other employees
833	Annealers, hardeners, temperers (metal)	6	4	4	6	5	6
834	Electroplaters, galvanisers, colour coaters	6	4	4	6	5	6
839	Other metal making and treating process operatives n.e.c.	6	4	4	6	5	6
840	Machine tool operatives (including CNC machine tool operatives)	6	4	4	6	5	6
841	Press stamping and automatic machine operatives	6	4	4	6	5	6
842	Metal polishers	6	4	4	6	5	6
843	Metal dressing operatives	6	4	4	6	5	6
844	Shot blasters	6	4	4	6	5	6
850	Assemblers/lineworkers (electrical/electronic goods)	6	4	4	6	5	6
851	Assemblers/lineworkers (vehicles and other metal goods)	6	4	4	6	5	6
859	Other assemblers/lineworkers n.e.c.	7	4	4	7	5	7
860	Inspectors, viewers and testers (metal and electrical goods)	5	4	4	5	5	5
861	Inspectors, viewers, testers and examiners (other manufactured goods)	5	4	4	5	5	5
862	Packers, bottlers, canners, fillers	7	4	4	7	5	7
863	Weighers, graders, sorters	7	4	4	7	5	7
864	Routine laboratory testers	3	4	4	3	2	3
869	Other routine process operatives n.e.c.	5	4	4	5	5	5
870	Bus inspectors	5	4	4	5	5	5
871	Road transport depot inspectors and related occupations	5	4	4	5	5	5
872	Drivers of road goods vehicles	7	4	4	7	5	7
873	Bus and coach drivers	7	4	4	7	5	7
874	Taxi, cab drivers and chauffeurs	4	4	4	7	5	7
875	Bus conductors	7	4	4	7	5	7
880	Seafarers (merchant navy); barge, lighter and boat operatives	6	4	4	6	5	6
881	Rail transport inspectors, supervisors and guards	5	4	4	5	5	5
882	Rail engine drivers and assistants	5	5	5	5	5	5
883	Rail signal operatives and crossing keepers	5	4	4	5	5	5
884	Shunters and points operatives	5	4	4	5	5	5
885	Mechanical plant drivers and operatives (earth moving and civil engineering)	7	4	4	7	5	7
886	Crane drivers	6	4	4	6	5	6
887	Fork lift and mechanical truck drivers	6	4	4	6	5	6
889	Other transport and machinery operatives n.e.c.	7	4	4	7	5	7
890	Washers, screeners and crushers in mines and quarries	5	4	4	5	5	5
891	Printing machine minders and assistants	6	4	4	6	5	6
892	Water and sewerage plant attendants	5	4	4	5	5	5
893	Electrical, energy, boiler and related plant operatives and attendants	6	4	4	6	5	6
894	Oilers, greasers, lubricators	6	4	4	6	5	6
895	Mains and service pipe layers, pipe jointers	7	4	4	7	5	7
896	Construction and related operatives	5	4	4	5	5	7
897	Woodworking machine operatives	6	4	4	6	5	6
898	Mine (excluding coal) and quarry workers	5	4	4	5	5	5
899	Other plant and machine operatives n.e.c.	6	4	4	5	5	6
900	Farm workers	6	4	4	6	2	6
901	Agricultural machinery drivers and operatives	6	4	4	6	5	6
902	All other occupations in farming and related	7	4	4	7	5	7
903	Fishing and related workers	4	4	4	7	5	7
904	Forestry workers	4	4	4	6	5	6
910	Coal mine labourers	7	4	4	7	5	7
911	Labourers in foundries	7	4	4	7	5	7
912	Labourers in engineering and allied trades	7	4	4	7	5	7
913	Mates to metal/electrical and related fitters	7	4	4	7	5	7
919	Other labourers in making and processing industries n.e.c.	7	4	4	7	5	7
920	Mates to woodworking trades workers	7	4	4	7	5	7
921	Mates to building trades workers	4	4	4	7	5	7
922	Rail construction and maintenance workers	5	4	4	5	5	5
923	Road construction and maintenance workers	5	4	4	6	5	6
924	Paviors, kerb layers	5	4	4	6	5	6
929	Other building and civil engineering labourers n.e.c.	7	4	4	7	5	7
930	Stevedores, dockers	7	4	4	7	5	7
931	Goods porters	7	4	4	6	5	7

Please note: This derivation table has no empty cells. See key at the end of table.

Table 17 - *continued*

Standard Occupational Classification 1990 unit group		Simplified NS-SEC	Employment status				
			1 Employers	2 Self-employed - no employees	3 Managers	4 Supervisors	5 Other employees
932	Slingers	7	4	4	7	5	7
933	Refuse and salvage collectors	7	4	4	7	5	7
934	Driver's mates	7	4	4	7	5	7
940	Postal workers, mail sorters	6	4	4	6	5	6
941	Messengers, couriers	6	4	4	6	5	6
950	Hospital porters	6	4	4	6	5	6
951	Hotel porters	7	4	4	7	5	7
952	Kitchen porters, hands	6	4	4	6	5	6
953	Counterhands, catering assistants	6	4	4	6	5	6
954	Shelf fillers	6	4	4	6	5	6
955	Lift and car park attendants	7	4	4	7	5	7
956	Window cleaners	4	4	4	7	5	7
957	Road sweepers	7	4	4	7	5	7
958	Cleaners, domestics	7	4	4	7	5	7
959	Other occupations in sales and services n.e.c.	7	4	4	7	5	7
990	All other labourers and related workers	7	4	4	7	5	7
999	All others in miscellaneous occupations n.e.c.	7	4	4	7	5	7

Please note: This derivation table has no empty cells.

Cells filled by the developers in April 2001.

Cells filled by using the priority order rules (see Appendix A).

Appendix A
A note on the derivation tables

Responses will sometimes produce combinations of codes for occupation and employment status/size of organisation that are incompatible or unallowable (for example, self-employed police officers).

When the original derivation tables were compiled, the cells for incompatible or unallowable combinations were left empty (see Table A1). For example, for SOC2000, all managerial jobs are in major group 1, which includes all the unit group codes that start with 1. In the original derivation tables, the cells in the employees' and supervisors' columns for unit groups in major group 1 were empty.

The tables in this user manual contain no empty cells because we have used priority order rules (shown in table a2) to fill them. Filling empty cells in this way does not make the combinations of codes allowable; it provides the best choice of NS-SEC value to use when these combinations of codes occur in data.

Applying priority order rules to fill the derivation tables

There are two ways of dealing with incompatible or unallowable responses in data processing systems:

- rejecting records and setting them aside for scrutiny by clerical staff, or

- automatically assigning a value to the records and so avoiding the need for clerical intervention.

The second method is used more often than the first. It requires derivation tables that have values in every cell. To achieve this for NS-SEC, analysts used the values in the allowable cells and data from the Labour Force Survey to devise the set of choices that form the priority order rules. The cells in the tables were then filled using the priority order rules.

The process of filling a derivation table is done one row at a time and working from left to right across the table.

- Where a cell is empty, we take the employment status/size of organisation given at the top of the column and use this code to identify which row of the priority order table we should use.

- Looking from left to right across the table, we take the number given in the first priority column.

- Using this number as an alternative employment status/size of organisation code, we return to our original row on the derivation table to locate the cell that sits in this column.

- If there is a value in this cell, this is the best alternative NS-SEC value to use for our original combination of codes and we write it into the original empty cell.

- But if the 'first priority' cell is empty, we return to the priority order table. Using our original employment status/size of organisation code to identify the correct row, we locate the number in the second priority column. Again, we use this number as an alternative employment status/size of organisation code and return to our original row on the derivation table to locate the cell that sits in this column. We repeat the process until we locate a cell that contains an NS-SEC value.

For example, to fill the empty cell on row 3213, under column 3, of the original NS-SEC derivation table, we would use row 3 of the priority order table (Table A2).

Table **A1**

Selected rows from the original NS-SEC full derivation table, operational categories, showing empty cells

SOC2000 unit group	ssec	Employment status/size of organisation						
		1	2	3	4	5	6	7
1162	5	1	8.1	9.1	5	5	-	-
3213	6	-	-	-	-	-	6	7.2
5312	9.1	1	8.1	9.1	-	-	10	13.3
6139	13.5	1	8.2	9.2	-	-	10	13.5
8114	11.2	1	8.1	9.1	-	-	10	11.2

ssec = simplified NS-SEC

The number in the first priority column is 2. Using 2 as an alternative employment status/size of organisation code, we return to the derivation table to look in row 3213, column 2. This cell is also empty. We return to row 3 of the priority order table to find our second priority code, which is 1. Column 1 of row 3213 of the derivation table also gives us a blank cell. Returning to row 3 of the priority order table, we find that the third priority code to use is 7. This returns us to the cell on row 3213, column 7, of the derivation table, which contains the value 7.2. We enter 7.2 into the original empty cell on row 3213, column 3.

Table A2

Priority order for choosing an alternative employment status/size of organisation code for the NS-SEC full derivation

Original employment status /size of organisation code	Priority					
	1st	2nd	3rd	4th	5th	6th
1	2	3	4	5	6	7
2	1	3	5	4	6	7
3	2	1	7	5	4	6
4	5	7	6			
5	4	7	6			
6	7	5	4			
7	5	4	6			

Table A3

Selected rows from the original NS-SEC full derivation table, operational categories, filled using the priority order table

SOC2000 unit group	ssec	Employment status/size of organisation						
		1	2	3	4	5	6	7
1162	5	1	8.1	9.1	5	5	5	5
3213	6	6	6	7.2	7.2	7.2	6	7.2
5312	9.1	1	8.1	9.1	13.3	13.3	10	13.3
6139	13.5	1	8.2	9.2	13.5	13.5	10	13.5
8114	11.2	1	8.1	9.1	11.2	11.2	10	11.2

ssec = simplified NS-SEC

Related publications

Available from:

Palgrave Macmillan
Houndmills
Basingstoke
Hampshire RG21 6XS
Tel: 01256 302611
www.palgrave.com/ons

Standard Occupational Classification 2000

Volume 1: Structure and description of unit groups

2000 Price £40 ISBN 0 11 621388 4

Volume 2: The coding index

2000 Price £39 ISBN 0 11 621389 2

Also available to download from www.statistics.gov.uk

The ESRC Review of Government Social Classifications

Published in 1998 jointly by ONS and ESRC, this report describes the development of the new socio-economic classification – the interim version of NS-SEC.

1998 Price £20 ISBN 1 85774 291 5

Also available to download from www.statistics.gov.uk

The National Statistics Socio-economic Classification: Origins, Development and Use

A complete description of the development of NS-SEC, including its rebasing on SOC2000.

2005 Price £50 ISBN 1 4039 9648 2

Also available to download from www.statistics.gov.uk

References

Elias, P., McKnight, A., Davies, R. and Kinshott, G. (2000) *Occupational Change: Revision of the Standard Occupational Classification*. Coventry: Institute of Employment Research, University of Warwick.

Erikson, R. (1984) 'Social Class of Men, Women and Families', *Sociology*, 18:4:500–514.

Erikson, R. and Goldthorpe, J.H. (1992). *The Constant Flux*. Oxford: Clarendon.

Goldthorpe, J.H. (1997) 'The 'Goldthorpe' class schema: some observations on conceptual and operational issues in relation to the ESRC review of government social classifications' in D. Rose and K. O'Reilly (eds) *Constructing Classes: Towards a New Social Classification for the UK*. Swindon: ESRC/ONS.

Goldthorpe, J.H. (with C. Llewellyn) (1980/1987) *Social Mobility and Class Structure in Modern Britain*. Oxford: Clarendon.

Government Statistical Service (1996) *Harmonised Concepts and Questions for Government Surveys*. London: ONS.

McCrossan, L. (1991) *A handbook for interviewers*. London: HMSO.

Marshall, G., Roberts, S., Burgoyne, C., Swift, A. and Routh, D. (1995) 'Class, Gender and the Asymmetry Hypothesis', *European Sociological Review*, 11:1:1–15.

Martin, J. (1995) 'Defining a Household Reference Person', *Survey Methodology Bulletin*, 37:1–7.

Martin, J. (1998) 'A New Definition for the Household Reference Person', *Survey Methodology Bulletin*, 43:1–8.

Martin, J. and Barton, J. (1996) 'The Effect of Changes in the Definition of the Household Reference Person', *Survey Methodology Bulletin*, 38:1–8.

Office for National Statistics (1998) *Inter Departmental Business Register: A Brief Guide*. London: ONS.

Office for Population Censuses and Surveys (1991) *Standard Occupational Classification, Volume 3: Social Classifications and Coding Methodology*. London: HMSO.

Rose, D. and O'Reilly, K. (eds) (1997) *Constructing Classes: Towards a New Social Classification for the UK*. Swindon: ESRC/ONS.

Rose, D. and O'Reilly, K. (1998) *The ESRC Review of Government Social Classifications: Final Report*. Swindon: ESRC/ONS.

Rose, D., O'Reilly, K. and Martin, J. (1997) 'The ESRC Review of Government Social Classifications', *Population Trends*, 89, Autumn 1997, 49–59.

Rose, D. and Pevalin, D. (2000) 'Social Class Differences in Mortality using the National Statistics Socio-economic Classification – Too Little, Too Soon: A Reply to Chandola', *Social Science and Medicine*, 51:1121–1127.

Rose, D. and Pevalin, D. (with O'Reilly, K.) (2005) *The National Statistics Socio-economic Classification: Origins, Development and Use*. London: ONS.

Glossary

ESRC Economic and Social Research Council The UK's leading research agency addressing economic and social concerns.

HRP Household Reference Person The person within the household who is chosen to characterise the household's social position. The official definition was introduced in 2001.

ISCO 88 International Standard Classification of Occupations 1988 The classification of occupations developed by the International Labour Office and revised in 1988.

ISCO 88 (COM) International Standard Classification of Occupations 1988 (COM) Eurostat commissioned this variant of ISCO 88 to improve the comparison of statistics on occupations across the countries of the European Union.

NS-SEC National Statistics Socio-economic Classification The new classification, with a defined conceptual basis, that has been developed to replace SC and SEG.

OUG Occupational Unit Group A group within the most detailed tier of the occupational classification, more specifically one of the 353 unit groups of the Standard Occupational Classification 2000.

SC Social Class based on Occupation (formerly Registrar General's Social Class) A scale for classifying people into five groups (represented by roman numerals), one subdivided. The composition of the classes brought together, as far as possible, people with similar levels of occupational skill. The allocation of occupations varied when Social Class was rebased on the revised occupational classification with the intention of preserving the gradient rather than literal continuity. It was derived from occupational unit group and employment status. The final version was based on the 1990 edition of the Standard Occupational Classification.

SEG Socio-economic Group The classification aimed to bring together people with similar social and economic status into 17 groups, three subdivided. It was derived from occupational unit group, employment status and size of establishment. The final version was based on the 1990 edition of the Standard Occupational Classification.

SOC90 Standard Occupational Classification 1990 The UK's occupational classification first published in 1990 to provide one standard and replace two previous official classifications used by government.

SOC2000 Standard Occupational Classification 2000 The latest edition of the UK's official occupational classification, revised, updated and published in June 2000.

ssec Simplified NS-SEC.